A Writer's Life:
More Ups Than Downs

To Lisa Wydle,

My Friend,

Jim Shew's

Nov. 30, 2003

A Writer's Life: More Ups Than Downs

Jim Shevis

Writers Club Press

San Jose New York Lincoln Shanghai

A Writer's Life:
More Ups Than Downs

Writers Club Press
an imprint of iUniverse, Inc.

For information address:
iUniverse, Inc.
5220 S. 16th St., Suite 200
Lincoln, NE 68512
www.iuniverse.com

ISBN: 0-595-24604-4

Printed in the United States of America

"For Carol, Heidi, Holly, Andrew and Buster"

Contents

Acknowledgements

My sincere appreciation to Gerry Bell, who was a constant source of encouragement when support was needed. And to Dave Solomon, without whose editing skills the book would not have seen the light of day.

Introduction

As an author and journalist with 35 years' experience, I have written features, breaking news, magazine articles, ad copy and speeches. But this is my first book, a task I undertook with some trepidation.

Writing is hard work, and I was good at rationalizing. While working a day job and raising a family, I found it easy to put off the book. Now that I've left the 9 to 5 work world, I have no excuses. I've written a memoir.

If you're going to write the story of your life and career, you better have something to say. There are too many books out there to compete for the browser's attention.

In all humility, I believe I have something to say. It's that while life may seem unfair we can overcome adversities if we believe in ourselves. Don't get discouraged; keep on the sunny side of life.

Throughout much of my life, I've struggled with an inferiority complex. It has dogged me continually. Not until later in life did I understand the root cause of it—my father's addiction to alcohol and how I allowed that to shape my life.

Had I not grown up in an alcoholic environment, I believe I would have been happier and even more successful in my career. Even so, as things have turned out, I've had more ups than downs.

Jim Shevis
Herndon, Virginia

1

It Was Easy

I doubt that you could do it today. At least with such ease as I did. I mean, you couldn't just go up to the president of the United States, ask him for his autograph and expect to get it.

Not after what happened in Dallas. But this is what I did a scant two months before John F. Kennedy was gunned down, and it wasn't difficult at all. It was easy, too easy.

I simply went up to him and said, "May I have your autograph, Mr. President?" Hoping that it would make him more receptive to my request, I added: "I'm from Massachusetts too." Which was true; I grew up in Massachusetts, the home of the Kennedys.

Obligingly, he scribbled his name in ink on the title page of the book I handed him. He then gave the book back to me with that captivating grin that had carried him from a congressional seat in Boston to the pinnacle of political power.

Four years later, when I approached Lyndon Johnson, at a Washington function to ask for his autograph, an overly protective Secret Service agent—no doubt conditioned by the Kennedy assassination —firmly pushed me away.

The book that President Kennedy signed that September day in Wyoming was not just any book. It was a paperback copy of his best-selling *Profiles in Courage*. I had brought it with me in the chance that he might autograph the book.

I mused how fitting it would be to have his signature on the same page that poet Robert Frost had written his name two years earlier; the crusty, white-haired Frost spoke at Kennedy's inauguration in 1961. It also crossed my mind that, with their autographs, it might become a valuable collector's item some day.

PRESIDENT KENNEDY SURROUNDED BY PRESS REPRESENTATIVES
AND WELL WISHERS, LEAVES JACKSON LAKE LODGE AFTER AN
OVERNIGHT STAY AT THE RESORT ON SEPTEMBER 25, 1963. THE
AUTHOR IS TO KENNEDY'S LEFT, WEARING GLASSES AND
HOLDING A PEN IN HIS HAND.

Kennedy was in the middle of a five-day, cross-country tour of the nation's natural resources and conservation projects. He had stopped at Jackson Lake Lodge, a posh resort hotel at Grand Teton National Park in northwest Wyoming, for an overnight stay. (Some of the president's critics thought the trip more of a campaign swing than anything else; it was late September 1963 and the 1964 presidential race was already heating up.)

As a staff reporter for United Press International in Cheyenne, I had gone to the Tetons to help UPI White House correspondents Merriman Smith and Alvin Spivak cover the president's brief stopover. Smitty and Al filed the main stories; I wrote sidebars on the atmospherics of the president's visit.

With little of real substance to report, I found myself interviewing the waitress who served him on what Kennedy had for dinner the evening of his arrival. Because of the nation's fascination with the young president, there might be readers out there who would like to know such trivia, my UPI bosses thought.

(For the record, Kennedy dined on Nova Scotia salmon followed by roast prime rib of beef au jus with baked russet potato, broccoli sauce béarnaise, and heart of butter lettuce. For dessert, he had a strawberry tart and Black Forest cherry cake.)

Kennedy was in a good mood the next day as he prepared to leave; it was evident on his face as he ambled toward a limousine that would take him to a waiting helicopter. The helicopter would then take him to Jackson Hole airport, where he would leave for Great Falls, Montana, the next stop on the tour.

He seemed relaxed and reluctant to leave the crisp mountain air and the spectacular Teton Range that rose 12,000 feet in the distance behind him.

"How do you like Wyoming?" shouted someone in the crowd that had gathered to bid him farewell.

"It's magnificent, just magnificent," he said. "I'm coming back!"

Little could Kennedy or anyone else know that he would be cut down by an assassin's bullet on a Dallas street two months later, and unable to keep his promise.

Like millions of Americans and millions of others around the globe, I was shocked at the news November 22, 1963 that the leader of the free world—a graceful figure of a man who seemed to have everything life could offer—lay dead at 46.

I first learned of the assassination as I stepped from a Super Constellation aircraft returning a group of Wyoming reporters to Cheyenne from Moffett Field in California. We had gone there with Wyoming's secretary of state on a press junket.

The shots in Dallas had rung out while we were in the air and while the pilot may have had word of the assassination before we landed, he kept the news to himself. As we alighted from the plane, an excited Wyoming National Guard general informed us in hushed tones that Kennedy had been killed in a communist plot that threatened to overthrow the country.

(The House Select Committee on Assassinations reported in 1979 that it was unlikely he was the victim of a communist conspiracy; but, the panel said, organized crime may have been involved.)

I hailed a taxi and rushed to UPI's cramped office on the second floor of the *Wyoming Tribune* building to write the following remembrance of the president's visit to the Cowboy State:

"He sat in the back of a black car, a boyish grin on his face. Secret Service men, anxious to get going, tried to move things along.

"Nearby, a Marine helicopter was ready to take him to Jackson Hole airport to board a plane that would carry him farther along on a tiring cross-country tour of the nation's natural resources and conservation projects.

"President Kennedy clearly was enjoying himself. And in the last few minutes of his overnight visit to Wyoming he was doing what he liked to do best: he was meeting the people.

"About 200 had turned out to bid him farewell at Jackson Lake Lodge, the Rockefeller-owned resort just inside Grand Teton National Park. He chatted with them, shook hands with all comers, and then departed. That was September 26.

"All the world today knows he won't be coming back, of course. John F. Kennedy, the 35th President of the United States, is dead."

2

Earlier Autographs

JFK's was not the first autograph I had obtained. Like many journalists, I had rubbed shoulders with a number of celebrities over the years and had collected a few of their signatures. Gradually over the years, I had a substantial collection.

Nine months before Kennedy's assassination, for example, I went backstage at the State Fair Music Hall in Dallas where Martin Luther King, Jr., was waiting to speak at a crowded voter-registration rally. I had joined UPI a month earlier, and had wanted to impress my new employer with an interview of the black civil-rights leader.

King was only moments away from addressing a waiting audience of 3,000 mostly blacks, however. Andrew Young, King's close friend and gatekeeper, politely signaled that there was no time for an interview. I understood the situation but before leaving I asked King for his autograph, which he graciously gave me.

The signature is in ink on a 2-3/4" by 3-1/2" sheet of white, lined notepad paper. It reads simply: "Best Wishes, Martin Luther King," without the "Jr." that distinguished him from his preacher father, Big Daddy King.

Then, too, I had obtained Frost's signature on the frontispiece of *Profiles in Courage* while attending the 1961 Bread Loaf Writers' Conference at Middlebury College in Vermont. Frost had helped found the annual conference in 1926.

But it was not until I had obtained Kennedy's signature that I began to take autograph collecting more seriously. Not as seriously as a professional autograph hound who collects and sells autographs for a living, but seriously enough so that over the next 30 years I managed to collect a significant number from well-known individuals in a variety of fields.

The Kennedy book increased in value—both sentimentally and monetarily—four years later when singer Marian Anderson signed her name next to Frost's and Kennedy's. The celebrated contralto, who had sung the national anthem at Kennedy's inaugural ball, was being toasted at a Washington awards luncheon in her honor.

In addition to those mentioned above, the collection includes the signatures of writer Norman Cousins; Vice President Al Gore; labor leaders George Meany, Lane Kirkland, and Douglas Fraser; journalists Walter Lippmann, Harrison Salisbury, Tom Gjelten, Walter Cronkite, Larry King, Deborah Norville, and Bob Woodward; comedians Flip Wilson, Vic Tayback, and Danny Thomas; singer Mary Wilson; guitarist Charlie Byrd; Soviet dissidents and human-rights advocates Andrei Sakharov, Yuri Orlov, and Andrei Amalrik; Chinese astrophysicist and dissident Fang Lizhi; former Costa Rican President Rodrigo Carazo; Under Secretary of Defense Frank G. Wisner; baseball players Hank Aaron, Bob Feller and Al Bumbry; Congressman Joseph P. Kennedy II; Chairman Colin Powell of the Joint Chiefs of Staff, later to become U.S. Secretary of State; Desert Storm hero General Norman Schwarzkopf; presidential candidate contenders Jesse Jackson and Pat Buchanan; General Barry R. McCaffrey (ret.), former director of the White House Office of Drug Control Policy; Secretary of State John Foster Dulles; Secretary of Labor Maurice J. Tobin; consumer advocate Esther Peterson; former Washington Redskins football coach Joe Gibbs, Redskins quarterback Joe Theisman and Redskins pass receiver Art Monk; vice presidential candidate Geraldine A. Ferraro; Presidents Jimmy Carter and George Bush; U.S. Ambassadors Jeane Kirkpatrick, Morris B. Abram, and John Kenneth Galbraith; U.S. Senators John Glenn, Charles Grassley and Paul Coverdell; First Ladies Barbara Bush and Lady Bird Johnson; actors Adam (Batman) West and Angie Dickinson; authors Michael Crichton and Cheryl Landon Wilson; investment broker Julius Westheimer and Israeli leaders Abba Eban and Ariel Sharon.

There are others, but those listed above were standouts in various fields of endeavor: politics, government, entertainment, sports, labor, journalism, human rights, and the military. Some may be less familiar to you than others; but each ranked high as a celebrity or newsmaker in their particular field.

More about autographs and autograph collecting in later chapters.

3

Family of Origin

I was born on October 2, 1929 in Brattleboro, Vermont, a town of about 8,000 people on the Connecticut River near the Massachusetts and New Hampshire borders. I am a New England Yankee by origin, then, even though I have lived longer in Virginia than anywhere else.

I am also a first-generation American of Scottish roots. Both my parents were born and raised in coastal villages in Scotland. This, plus the fact that I grew up in New England, explains a lot about my character and my personality, I believe. People are largely a product of their environment. Scots tend to be introspective, New Englanders taciturn. These traits, which I came by honestly, stamped my formative years.

There was an even stronger influence in my early life, which I will go into at greater length later for the importance it played in my life. That influence was the effect my father's drinking had upon me and other members of the family. My nephew, a major in the Marine Corps looking into his own family roots, once asked me what I thought was the operative "dynamic" of the Shevis family. It was, I said without hesitation, "alcohol."

Adult children of alcoholics (ACOAs) reading this will know what I mean. Children raised in an alcoholic environment don't talk about the important things in their lives; they don't trust others for fear of getting hurt, and they don't feel their feelings—they stuff them inside where they'll be safe from the inconsiderations and insensitivities of others.

These "don'ts" applied to me as I grew up. After counseling and attending many 12-step meetings, however, I believe that I have largely overcome these character defects. But their stamp on me at a very early age left a lasting mark on me, my siblings and, of course, my mother. Ironically, never thinking I would follow my father's example, in later years I turned to alcohol myself to solve my problems.

My father, James Allan Shevis, was a decent man. He did as well as he could, given the trauma of his own upbringing and the times in which our family lived. His drinking never got in the way of his work, and he provided well enough for us all during the years of the Great Depression. I think he loved his children; he just didn't know how to express his feelings properly.

My mother, Frances Isobel Walker Ritchie Shevis, was a warm, outgoing and spirited woman, a good storyteller with an excellent command of the English language. Women friends would come to the house for afternoon tea, and she would read their fortunes in the tea leaves; invariably they would leave happier than when they arrived.

She was a musical person, too, an attribute she inherited from her father, Joseph Ritchie, a man eulogized at his death as "one of the most talented musicians Peterhead (Scotland) has ever produced." I fondly recall the tunes she would play on the family upright piano; she could play any song she had ever heard once. Along with her brothers, she played in her father's six-piece orchestra at one time or another at different venues in Scotland.

I know less about my mother's family than I do about my father's. I do know, however, that the Ritchies were well educated, accomplished people. Her brother Jack served as a major on General Bernard Montgomery's staff in the North African campaign during World War Two. Her other brother Alec was proprietor of a store in Aberdeen, I believe. Her sister Jean married an Englishman, Percy Wolstencroft, a British civil servant who spent most of his career in Gibraltar.

My father's side of the family were primarily tradesmen, seafarers, and soldiers. My mother's side of the family were primarily scholars and intellectuals. As time marched on and higher education became more available to all, both sides produced a bumper crop of Ph.D's. While I seem to have inherited or acquired many of the characteristics of my father's family, I have my mother's love of music and storytelling.

My father was born in the fishing village of Fraserburgh on Scotland's eastern coast; my mother was born in nearby Peterhead, today the center of extensive oil-drilling operations in the North Sea. Each would bicycle half the seven-mile distance between them to picnic, to have what my mother would call "a good claque" (talk), or to do whatever else lovers do when courting. They were both so young, only in their late teens, she two years younger than he; I can see them now, waving to each other at their appointed meeting place overlooking the rugged Scottish coastline, happy to see each other.

Many years later, in early September 1997, my son Andrew and I visited Fraserburgh so that he might better know his ancestral roots. At Kinnaird's Head, we clambered over huge boulders that jut out into the sea just as my father did when he was a boy, and visited the sandy beach near his home he often talked about. It was a moving experience for both of us.

As we ended our Fraserburgh visit, Andy said: "It looks like a tough town." His observation was right on the mark, a tough town it is to this day.

4

What's in a Name?

*"What's in a name? That which we call a rose
"By any other name would smell as sweet."*

—— Juliet, in Shakespeare's "Romeo and Juliet"

Shevis is a rare name, even in Scotland where the country's national telephone directory lists only a handful of people by that name. I often wondered where it came from.

In the United States, there aren't many more Shevises than there are in all of Scotland. It's not a name you'll find on every street corner. But genealogy buff that I am, I've uncovered some fascinating history about the name.

My mother's maiden name, Ritchie, is as common in Scotland as Smith or Jones are in America. I like the name Ritchie: if that were my name, I wouldn't have to constantly correct people who want to pronounce Shevis any way but the correct way. Also, Ritchie is readily identifiable as a Scottish name and I am proud of my heritage.

Shevis, on the other hand, neither looks nor sounds like a Scottish name. It looks as if it should be pronounced "SHE-vis" with the accent on the first syllable. Hispanics seem to think it should be pronounced as "SHAW-vez" while Jewish people want to pronounce it "SHE-vitz." Me? I think it's simple to pronounce: it rhymes with "crevice." Properly pronounced, it even has a graceful lilt to it.

Over the years, I have collected a slew of facts about the Shevis family—enough to convince me of my roots—and probably have more

15

information about the name and those who have borne it than anyone else.

My curiosity about the origin of the name heightened when my son Andrew was born in 1970. I wanted to be able to pass on to him as much knowledge of his ancestry as possible.

Shortly after Andy's birth, I wrote to the General Wine and Spirits Company in New York for any information they might have to link the Chivas Regal Scotch name to mine. Chivas and Shevis seemed so similar, I thought there had to be a connection. Chivas Regal, which the company imported into the United States, is regarded by drinkers of Scotch as the best on the market.

Jerome A. Newman, who was president of the company at the time, replied that for 13 years he had been gathering information about the name Chivas for a book about the whisky he planned to publish. When he completed the research, he said, he would supply me with the information.

I never heard from him, even though I wrote him again, but he did note in his letter: "I can tell you now that the motto, coat of arms, and tartan have been lost during the many centuries of the Chivas family history and my endeavors in attempting to locate them have been fruitless."

So much for hopes of finding a financial link between General Wine and Spirits and me in the event I was searching for one, which I was not. Yet I felt sure that the names Chivas and Shevis had a common root.

A magazine ad for the whisky, headed "P.C.R.—or Pronouncing Chivas Regal is easier than producing it"—abounded in clues to the origin of the family name that I was later able to confirm. The copy read as follows:

"Unless you're related to the family, you may mispronounce the first word in Chivas Regal (Scotland's Prince of Whiskies). It rhymes with 'give us.'

"We have been asked, 'How does a Scottish distiller happen to have such a French-looking name?' The name is pure Scots, but its present spelling is the result of the free and easy attitude toward spelling which was customary in the Middle Ages.

"In the 14th century, the family gave its name to (or took it from) the hamlet of Shivas in the parish of Tarves, Aberdeenshire. For generations you could take your choice of *Shivas, Schivas, Schevas, or Seves*. Somebody who liked the letter 'C' settled on *Chivas*, long before 1801. That was the year when two brothers Chivas set up in Aberdeen as 'purveyors of provisions.'

"They purveyed with such success that they were able to give serious and scholarly attention to the development of one 'provision', which made them famous. They acquired consummate skill in blending fine whisky. Soon they were producing a liquid treasure so delectable that a London journalist wrote, 'we have never tasted finer, mellower, and more exquisitely flavoured whisky than that which Chivas Brothers hospitably placed before us during our sojourn in Aberdeen'."

About the same time, I sent away to the Scots Ancestry Research Society in Edinburgh for a report on my father's side of the family. The report traced my father's maternal ancestry, but only back to 1805; I wanted to go farther back than that.

The report recounted my father's birth in Fraserburgh on May 1,1897 to Helen Allan and Andrew Sheves, who were married in Fraserburgh on December 30, 1887 at the ages of 18 and 19, respectively. The entry listed my grandfather's occupation at the time of the marriage as a (journeyman) cooper, and my grandmother's as a domestic servant.

Then one day, on a business trip to Boston in 1974, I happened upon a used-book store on Newbury Street and came across George F. Black's *The Surnames of Scotland* (New York Public Library, NY, 1946.) The discovery marked the first major find in my quest for knowledge about the origin of the Shevis name.

The entry for *Shivas, Shives, Chives* listed two dozen spelling variations and went back nearly 600 years. It thrilled me to know that the name had survived in one form or another all those years. An even greater thrill was knowing that these were *my* people, for the most part ordinary folks who had come and gone on their travels on this earth, just as I.

One of the spellings, *Sheves*, was identical to that of my father's when he came to the United States. Why he changed the second "e" to "i" I'll never know for sure; he once told me, however, that his employer, the Boston and Maine Railroad, spelled it that way on his time sheet and he decided to leave it like that.

Because of the importance I attached to this discovery, I include it here in its entirety:

"Shivas, Shives, Chives. Of territorial origin from the old barony of the name in the parish of Tarves, Aberdeenshire. John Sheves, scholar in Scotland, had a safe conduct to study in Scotland, 1393. Andrew Schewas appears in Aberdeen, 1408.

"William Scheues, 'an accomplished physician and astrologer,' ignorant of theology, coadjutor bishop of St. Andrews, became archbishop in 1477. John Scheves, a follower of the earl of Cassilis, was respited for murder in 1526. Bessie Schives, spouse of Robert Blinschell, 1596. John Scives, trade burgess of Aberdeen, 1647.

"Mr. James Shives was professor of philosophy, 1648, and James *Chivas*, shipmaster, Fraserburgh, 1759.

"Cheivies, 1685; Chevis, 1696; Chivish, 1652; Schevys, 1477; Schewas, 1512; Schewess, 1476; Schivis, 1689; Schiviz, 1685; Sevas, 1473; Schawes, 1521; Sheifas, 1768; Chevis, Chives, Civis, Schevaes, Scheviz, Shevas, *Sheves*, Shivis, Seves, Sivis."

But the best was yet to come in my search for connection and identity. During our 1997 visit to Scotland, my son and I stopped in St. Andrews, a university town rich in culture and tradition where the game of golf is said to have first been played around 1400 A.D.

After a round of golf on one of the courses of the renowned Royal and Ancient Golf Club, we set off for the House of Schivas, a 15th-century castle near Tarves that I had read about in a book my mother had given me years earlier.

The Book of Buchan, which was published privately in Aberdeen in 1943, contains a chapter about this magnificent tower house. I had often fancied that it was *my* castle, not some rich English laird's. So in planning our trip, I had written its current occupant, Innes Catto, if we might visit him and perhaps be given a tour of the baronial estate.

Catto not only consented to give us a tour of the property but also gave us a detailed, written history of the Chivas family dating back to the 11th century.

The opening lines blew my mind for their historical significance:

"The family Schevez was of Norman origin. They arrived in England in the army of William the Conqueror (1066) and led their contingent at Hastings."

Imagine having forbears who were there at one of the most fateful military engagements in history! And this, more than 900 years ago.

William's victory at Hastings paved the way for Norman subjugation of all England. It was the first and last time that England would ever be defeated.

According to the history, which had the ring of truth to it, the Schevez family's arrival in Scotland dates from the reign of David I (1124–1153), David invited the Norman barons of England to settle in Scotland. These Norman barons first settled in the southern districts of the country on grants of land given to them by the king. This process gradually spread northward, and in the passage of time the family assumed ownership of the Barony of Schevez in the 14th century.

There was more in this intriguing document that went to the core of my search. What I had been looking for was the etymology of the name Shevis—the word itself—and the meaning behind it. The family history had a plausible answer:

"The name Schevez is of territorial origin, represented by the old Barony of Schivas in the parish of Tarves, Aberdeenshire. The Celtic people, who named so many of the physical features of Scotland and the Northeast gave the name 'seamhas', meaning 'prosperity', to the territory that afterwards became known as the Barony of Schivas."

This was a real find, I thought, somewhat akin to the discovery of the Titanic, on a much smaller level, of course. It could explain the spelling variations of my name over the centuries. (Pronounce the word "seamhas" [SHAY-muss] and you'll find it not too much of a stretch for "seamhas" to have evolved to "Chivas," "Schevez"—or Shevis.)

And how nice to think that your name may have derived from a root meaning "success" or "good fortune."

Enough of the Dark and Middle Ages. Yet, what is past is prologue.

5

Granny

Significantly, my father grew up in an alcoholic home. His father, Andrew, was the drinker and by all accounts weak-willed; he died in his 60's. Helen Allan, his wife, can best be described as a shrew, who dominated not only her husband but also her four sons; she died just short of her 101st birthday.

I met my grandmother twice. I was just a boy. Once, in the late 1930s, she visited us at our home in Hoosick Falls, New York. Her second visit came at the end of World War Two; we were living in Gardner, Massachusetts then. My father was very fond of her, and deferred to her at all times, as I recall. My mother, on the other hand, did not like her: she felt that Granny thought she was not good enough for her son.

Besides my father, Helen and Andrew had three other sons, Gordon, William and George. William died in London, an alcoholic, I was told. According to my parents, George suffered a motorcycle accident while serving with the British Army in India and died in a mental institution as a result.

Gordon served in the British merchant marine most of his life, and traveled the world. Later in life, he married and settled down in Fraserburgh. I remember his brief stay with us in Gardner after the Second World War. For some strange reason, I became mesmerized as I watched him shave one day. He said he used cold water only because that's what he had got used to as a sailor.

In my first trip to Scotland, in the summer of 1977, I spent a weekend at Uncle Gordon's home in Fraserburgh. By then, he was hard of

21

hearing, which made conversation difficult, but he seemed pleased with my visit. I had gone to Britain for a three-week course on modern British economics and politics at Cambridge University. Gordon and his wife Bella met me at the railway station in Aberdeen, where the line ended, and we drove the 40 miles to Fraserburgh in his car.

Like my father, Uncle Gordon had grown up in awe of his termagant mother while Bella shared my mother's intense dislike for her. Granny had passed away a few years earlier, and Gordon spoke freely of her.

On a tour of northeast Scotland in his car, Gordon drove us to his mother's gravesite in Keith. As we drove past lavender fields of heather and gorse, he told me a delightful story of how my grandmother fought the Luftwaffe singlehandedly. One day early in World War Two, German planes flew over Fraserburgh, dropping their bombs close to her home on Charlotte Street.

"She was so angry," Gordon said, "and so protective of her home that she took her rifle, climbed up on the roof and fired at them, not caring that she might have made herself a target." Whether her shooting had any effect on the enemy is not known, but it made her feel good to know that she had done something to defend her property, Gordon said.

6

After the War: America

A t the age of 17, my father went off to war. The year was 1914. He came home four years later, no longer a callow youth but a rebellious young man who had witnessed bloody fighting in France and Belgium. In later years, after he had immigrated to the United States, he spoke little of his wartime experiences except to say that he had seen the Red Baron shot down. Baron von Manfred Richthofen, the German flying ace credited with destroying 80 Allied planes, was downed behind British lines in April 1918. My father, who claimed to have watched the shootdown, said that Richthofen no sooner landed his bullet-ridden aircraft than soldiers swarmed over the plane for souvenirs.

The only other event he spoke about that I can recall, was Germany's use of mustard gas against the British at Ypres, Belgium in July 1917. Mustard gas (or dichloroethyl sulfide) blinded its victims and produced a blistering skin and bleeding lungs.

Because of his reticence to talk about that awful period of world history, I am not exactly sure what my father did during "the war to end all wars." But from snippets of his conversation, I believe it had something to do with laying lines of communication. He may even have been what was called a "sapper," someone who detonates unexploded bombs. Before entering the army, he had worked for a telephone company in Scotland and that may have qualified him for that kind of work in the military.

In any event, when he returned home in 1918, weary of years of army discipline and wartime living conditions, he dreamt of going to

23

America for a better future. I once asked him why he decided to leave Scotland; he said he made the decision the day his supervisor at the phone company insisted that he address him as "sir." That apparently was the last straw. My father had had enough of that in the army; he decided to strike out on his own.

By then, he and my mother had married and she had given birth to a baby boy, Joseph, who died when he was but six weeks old. The loss, along with the trauma of the war, may also have contributed to his decision to leave Scotland. Promising to send for my mother as soon as he earned money for her passage, he packed his bags and sailed off to America.

Like millions of others who came to our shores, he passed through immigration services at Ellis Island where, as he tells the story, he had a burning desire to go to the bathroom. In his haste, he ran into the ladies' room only to be greeted by female shrieks. "I thought the sign said 'laddies' room'," he said. A perfectly natural mistake for a laddie from Scotland to make.

From New York, he went to Boston where he had relatives and landed a job with the Boston and Maine Railroad's signal department in Brattleboro, Vermont. He worked the next 42 years for the B & M, retiring at the age of 65. Six months after his arrival in the United States, he sent money for my mother's passage. They were now in the land of the free and the home of the brave—and happy to be there. Their new life had just begun.

I have often thought that one of the best things my parents ever did was to come to the United States. Had they not, I would not have had the opportunity to succeed as well as I have. Britain in the early 20th century still had its class system; America was not class-conscious.

I can see now it was a courageous thing they did. They were only in their 20s, he three years her senior, both with little formal education. He went only to the eighth grade, my mother to the seventh. It took courage to leave family and friends behind to start a new life in a foreign country.

7

Brattleboro

All five of us children—Margaret, Frances, Jean, Gordon and me—were born in Brattleboro, a bucolic community in Vermont where English poet Rudyard Kipling lived for a time. Another boy, Donald, was born in Gardner but died of a vitamin K deficiency a day or two after his birth. I was the middle child, closer in age to Jean than to the others. Jean was 18 months younger than I, Frances 21 months older, Margaret six years older, and Gordon six years younger.

One of my earliest memories was the day my parents brought my infant brother, Gordon, home from the hospital. I was six years old; we were living in a three-bedroom, stucco house in Brattleboro. It was an exciting moment for all of us and I sensed something of the miraculous in this squalling bundle of humanity.

Another early Brattleboro memory was sitting in my little rocking chair (which I still have) next to my father's rocker, pretending to read the weekly newspaper, the *Brattleboro Reformer*. I was four years old, and would look up to him to see if he were watching me. I was simply mimicking him. Someone once said that there is in every man a boy trying to please his father. That's what I was trying to do, even though I felt I never succeeded.

After 15 years in Brattleboro, the B & M transferred my father to Hoosick Falls, a rural community in upstate New York near Troy and Albany. The year was 1936, and the nation was at the height of the Great Depression. I had just completed first grade at Brattleboro's Oak Grove School, a block from our home at 1 Baldwin Street. Kansas Governor Alfred Landon was the Republican presidential candidate that year, opposing Franklin Delano Roosevelt. As they left school, the older kids would chant "We Want Landon, We Want Landon." I was too young to know what the political campaign was all about. (FDR won in a landslide; Landon carried only Vermont and Maine.)

I remember my parents loading the four-door Essex sedan with kids and suitcases, and heading west for Hoosick Falls along Vermont's Molly Stark Trail. We seemed a happy lot, my mother leading us in singing "She'll Be Coming 'Round the Mountain When She Comes," and my father urging us to "Remember: You'll always be Vermonters."

8

My Dad

But we were not a happy lot. We were in denial. Children who grow up in an alcoholic home have a great capacity for denial. It was only much later in life, after my wife had left me, that I could conclude my father was an alcoholic and that his illness had affected us all.

There is a widely held theory among psychologists called "family systems" that explains alcohol's effect not only on the alcoholic but also on those around the drinker. The theory holds that the illness or predisposition to drink is passed on from generation to generation. I think it definitely applied to my family.

Alcoholism, it seems to me, is a worldwide problem. In the United States, it is particularly widespread. According to the National Institute on Alcohol Abuse and Alcoholism, about one in four children in the United States is exposed to family alcoholism or alcohol abuse while growing up.

There are an estimated 14-million alcoholic Americans. Alcoholism is believed to be caused by a mix of genetic and environmental factors, and studies have shown children of alcoholics, such as me and my siblings, are at an increased risk.

By the time of his transfer to Hoosick Falls, my father was drinking heavily. An episodic drinker, he never missed a day's work; he did most of his drinking on weekends and holidays. I remember him coming home late one night in Brattleboro, ranting and raving and chasing my mother around the house. I was no more than five or six years old at the time. I remember the absolute terror I felt as she fled with my sisters and me to the attic to get away from him. All I remember after that

27

was his yelling names at her and his turning the light at the foot of the stairs on and off.

His drinking progressively worsened and continued throughout his life to varying degrees; in his 90's he said he was down to one or two drinks a day. He never saw himself as an alcoholic. None of us knew what to do about his drunken behavior; we thought all families were like this. Jean and I even began to believe that we were responsible for his drinking. We would say to each other, as if to absolve ourselves, "We didn't ask to be born."

It was a terrible experience. My mother, who did not drink at all, knew the damage alcohol was doing to the family but with five young children to care for and no place to turn she felt trapped. Unlike women today, she felt she could not just up and leave.

Once, when I had done something to displease him, my father lit into me so badly, it caused my mother to intervene. "Stop," she said. "Don't you know what you're doing to that boy?" she said. On earlier occasions, in a drunken state, he drew red welts on my body with a leather strop.

9

Hoosick Falls

All of this had a predictable effect on me. I withdrew unto myself, distrusted people, and lived in fear. I had poor self-esteem. I felt unloved. While I excelled in school, my social development suffered. I wet the bed nightly and stuttered until I went to high school. My mother frequently failed to change the bedclothes either because she tired of it or simply forgot, and I would have to sleep on a wet mattress night after night. You can imagine the shame I felt. The signs were clear, but totally ignored: I was a troubled young boy. These signs would become manifest in years to come, however, when they could not be ignored.

I long ago forgave my father for the fear and shame he instilled in his children. It was his sickness. It wasn't my dad. He could be gentle when he was not drinking.

Further, we reach a point in life when it does no good to lay blame on someone else no matter how badly they have treated us. We learn that we need to take responsibility for our own lives, and move on.

The happiest days of my boyhood, despite my father's abuse of alcohol—and the abuse of his family that went with the drinking—were the four years we spent in Hoosick Falls. In 1936, when we moved there, America was still rural and life a lot less complicated than today.

A neighbor, Albert Farqhuarson, who was about four years older than I, sort of adopted me and would take me with him Saturday mornings to hunt and shoot squirrels. I'd always wanted a squirrel's tail, but I could never kill animals for sport. I feel that way even today.

As a result, I never got a squirrel's tail, but I enjoyed the hike through the meadows with Albert.

A great source of fun was joining other neighborhood kids in jumping into a pile of hay from the loft of a barn near our house. The barn was owned by a farmer who would chase us away with a pitchfork when he saw us playing there. We, of course, would taunt the poor man. I remember to this day how courageous I felt when I stood up to him—albeit from some distance off—and later bragged to my mother about how brave I was.

Our wood-frame house at 18 Renssalaer Street was situated near the top of a steep hill. The location made for perfect sledding in the wintertime; it was downhill all the way to the Cheney Free Public Library and Classic Street School that we attended.

Most Saturday mornings, we would go to the library to hear a librarian read stories to us. One particular story that stands out in my memory was that about Little Black Sambo and the tiger that chased him. Back then, in 1938, nobody seemed to think there was anything racist about the story. Today, Little Black Sambo is seen as a symbol of racism in America and the book banned from most libraries.

Autumn in Hoosick Falls, with its crisp air and the brilliant reds and yellows of the foliage, was absolutely beautiful. I felt really alive then. In front of our house were two horse-chestnut trees, which dropped their nuts on the lawn in the autumn. What fun we had cracking them open for their meat or to string them into chains and necklaces.

On Sundays, my mother would send us downtown to the First Presbyterian Church for Sunday School, a mile or so away. It was at the church that I got to know more about Jesus. I loved the hymns, especially "Fairest Lord Jesus," "The Old Rugged Cross," and "Jesus Loves Me, This I Know," I felt secure there, and the church's activities for children were fun.

I don't recall my father ever attending the church, and my mother went there only rarely; she just couldn't get away from household chores or my father's demands upon her. She was a professed Christian, however, and I remember her favorite hymn was "Onward Christian Soldiers." I think my father was a Christian, too, though I don't recall that he ever expressed his religious beliefs. At the end of his life, as he lay dying in a nursing home, he told me that he prayed every day.

My parents liked Hoosick Falls. It had a sizable Scottish community that they blended in with easily; the number was large enough to support a Scottish-American clan—Clan MacIntosh—that my father served as chieftain at one time. But he continued to abuse alcohol, and that led to arguments with my mother that instilled fear among us children.

One night when, home alone, I answered a knock at the door to find a towering police officer—his name was Mooney—standing there wanting to know my father's whereabouts. I was terrified. I had no idea where my father was, and the officer soon left. Dad had been drinking and verbally abusing my mother; she had called the police and fled with my brother and sisters, leaving me behind for some reason.

His drinking episodes were worse on weekends and holidays. Social events at Clan MacIntosh, such as the clan's annual Christmas party, centered on alcohol and invariably deteriorated into drunken arguments and fights between my parents. As innocent and defenseless children, we felt beaten by something over which we had no control. Psychologists have likened the impact of alcoholic behavior on those around the drinker to that experienced by Vietnam War veterans; they call it "post-traumatic stress syndrome."

Materially, our family was lucky. My father, a member of the Brotherhood of Railway Signalmen, an AFL-CIO labor union, had a secure job that enabled him to support the family throughout the Depression. We always had food and clothes to wear. Others were not as fortunate.

I never thought of us as being poor. My father would come home after work on payday, Thursday, and settle up with my mother, giving her money to pay the bills. (She always thought he shortchanged her, holding back money for himself to buy beer and liquor; she was probably right.)

Jean and I would each get a one-or-two-cent "allowance." Margaret and Frances got three or four cents because they were the oldest children. Gordon's penny was held in trust for him by my mother since he was too young to appreciate money.

What could you buy for one or two cents? Well, you could buy candy or a favor at the nearby grocery store—one cent, for instance, would get you three or four pieces of hard rock candy—or you could save or pool your resources until you had a dime or a quarter, which gave you other buying options.

In 1949, as a junior at the University of Massachusetts, I wrote about this weekly ritual for a creative-writing class. The assignment was to recreate a childhood experience. I called it, "Allowance Day":

"What fun we had, Jean and I. Of my three sisters, I felt closest to her, probably because we were only 18 months apart. Anything but rich, we took joy from life in the simplest way and tried to be content with what we had.

"I fondly recall those happy Thursday afternoons when Dad steamed up Renssalaer Street in his 1929 Essex; sometimes he had to leave the car at the bottom of the hill and hike home because the steep was so great.

"On those days, when all seemed well with the world, Dad and the Essex, Jean and I were filled with excitement. For Thursday was Allowance Day. As soon as he settled with my mother for the bills that had to be paid, my father lined up the five of us and gave each our weekly allowance. He would jingle the coins in his hands—mostly pennies and nickels—and then, starting with Margaret, the oldest child, press a coin, sometimes two or three, in each of the hands that stuck out eagerly. Jean and I were each given two pennies while Frances and Margaret were given three cents, or sometimes a whole nickel.

"Five-year-old Gordon didn't get an allowance, really. A penny was put into his chubby fist but it stayed there only a minute or two. Mother saved his allowance money in a specially built piggy bank, which Jean and I used to fondle with awe.

"With four cents between us, Jean and I felt like two of the richest kids in the world. These were the days when money was worth double or triple today's value. For a penny, we could buy a flat piece of bubble gum wrapped in colorful wax paper, with a picture card of some horrible scene from the Sino-Japanese war enclosed within. Jean and I had a hundred or more of these cards in our collection, and were the envy of the neighborhood.

"After we had gotten our allowance, we busied ourselves planning what to do with it. Margaret and Frances usually spent theirs on candy or ice cream but Jean and I nearly always pooled our resources into some business transaction—such as the Christmas play that we staged.

"For four consecutive Allowance Days, Jean and I saved our pennies. A couple of days before Christmas, Dad gave each one of us an extra dime. Together, we had 36 cents—enough to buy decorations and refreshments for the play.

"The play was held on Christmas Eve. Jean and I were the principal actors. She played Mary, I played Joseph, and a doll was used to portray the infant Jesus. The neighbors were invited and on opening night there were 15 people in attendance.

"When the proceeds from the refreshment sales were totaled up, we had made $1.10. We could hardly wait for the next Allowance Day. We needed the four cents we expected to get for a New Year's party."

On Saturdays, to get us out of the house more than for any other reason, we'd each get 10 cents for the movies; the theater always showed a double feature plus shorts. One of the films was always a cowboy movie. Hopalong Cassidy, Charles Starrett, Andy Devine, Roy Rogers and Gene Autry were my favorite cowboys. Often, when we got home, there'd be the drinking and arguing; we never knew what to expect or when the fighting would start up again.

10

Grandma Moses

A town of about 2,500 people, Hoosick Falls was virtually unknown until the painter Grandma Moses was "discovered" there in 1940. A New York City art dealer passing through saw her paintings on display in a downtown store.

A farm wife, with no formal art training, she began painting in her 70's. Her primitives are colorful, simple, and carefree scenes of rural life—many of them set in Hoosick Falls. When I look at her work, I am brought back to the time when I lived in Hoosick Falls; the rolling meadows and farmland of the area are indelibly fixed in my mind.

Grandma Moses died in 1961 at the age of 101 and was buried in Maple Grove Cemetery off Main Street extension in Hoosick Falls—a cemetery that looks like her paintings come to life. A series of markers leads visitors to the hilly site where her grave marker carries the simple epitaph, "Anna Mary Robertson Moses." Nearby, there runs a brook where I saw my first tadpole one fine spring day, causing me to think about the beauties and mysteries of nature. How could this little creature ever grow into a frog? I wondered.

My mother shared a hospital room with Moses in Cambridge, a small community near Hoosick Falls. My mother was there for a gallstones operation; I don't know the reason for Grandma Moses's hospitalization. According to my mother, the two of them regaled themselves with stories, which helped them keep up their spirits and stay positive-minded during their hospital stay.

11

Choosing a Career

Looking back on my life, I can see a pattern of turns and events that led me to choose journalism as a profession. I did not get into journalism by accident. I consciously prepared for it.

It started before I ever saw the inside of a classroom. My mother would read me stories from Grimm's fairy tales, Hans Christian Anderson and Thornton Burgess. (Thirty years later, as a newsman for United Press International, I interviewed Burgess in a Hamden, Massachusetts nursing home shortly before his death.) Thus, I got into the habit of reading early on. By the time I started school, I could read quite well. Reading, of course, is fundamental to learning and ever so to writing.

When we were seven and eight years old, respectively, Jean and I started a very primitive block newspaper, which we wrote by hand and delivered to a few houses in the neighborhood. It carried news such as what movie was playing downtown, what mischief our tomcat had gotten into, and who recently had visited the family. It fizzled out for lack of interest.

What clearly influenced my desire to become a newsperson, though, was a fifth-grade field trip to the Hoosick Falls weekly newspaper. When we went into the paper's back shop, a Linotype operator set each pupil's name in lead type. Seeing my name in type appealed to my ego, and I dreamed of seeing my name on a news story some day.

I was a good student, getting high marks in school. In grade school, the subjects I enjoyed most were those basic to a career in journalism—reading, writing and spelling. I also liked geography, and yearned to know more about foreign countries; I think this was because my parents had relatives in other parts of the world, and I wanted to know more about them and where they lived.

From the time I was eight or nine, there was little doubt in my mind about what I wanted to do with my life: I wanted to go into the news business. Listening to Lowell Thomas report on radio from such exotic places as Mongolia and Tibet stirred my sense of adventure. I wanted to go to faraway places, too.

While it is said today's college graduates may have as many as five careers during their lifetime, I wanted but one—journalism. It was an exciting field, a way of seeing the world and meeting people from all walks of life.

From time to time, I have been asked how do you prepare for a career in journalism. At Career Day at Herndon (Virginia) Middle School, where I have talked to students about journalism as a career, my answer has been, first of all, it helps to have a healthy curiosity about people, places and things around you. Almost any experience is grist for a journalist's mill, and often can be turned into an advantage unexpectedly at a later date.

Then, too, it helps to be able to detach when the world around you seems to be falling apart. Children of alcoholics have an edge in this respect in a perverse way. We learned early in life to detach from the craziness that an alcoholic parent inflicted on our lives. Journalists learn to detach from what they're covering in order to report truthfully and objectively. Getting good grades at school—but more important, really learning what you're studying—is an important qualification, especially for college.

If there is one skill that a would-be journalist must master today it is the fast-changing technology in the communications industry. Computer literacy is an essential qualification. The better acquainted you are with the Internet, Microsoft and other tools of the craft, the better positioned you are to succeed in this highly competitive field.

When it comes to college preparation for journalism—and a college degree is a *sine qua non* for a journalism career as it is in almost any career field—there are two main paths to choose from: attending a journalism school or pursuing a liberal-arts education. This is as true today as it was when I went to college. I chose to pursue a liberal-arts education, grounding myself in English and studying a wide range of other subjects—economics, political science, botany, music appreciation and literature to mention a few.

At the same time, I took every opportunity to write. Learning by doing is still the fast track to craft mastery. If I had my life to live over again, I would probably again choose to pursue a liberal-arts education. Why? I have always believed that a truly educated person is one who is well-rounded, knowledgeable and able to discourse on a wide variety of topics. A renaissance person, if you will.

Journalism schools tend toward the strictly utilitarian. Their focus is often narrow, concentrated on such subjects as writing a news lead, the limitations of the inverted pyramid, plagiarism, and ethics in journalism. While these are important things to know, I believe most intelligent people pick them up along the way. More important is knowing what you're writing about; for that you need a storehouse of information to tap when you're searching for just the right quote or epigraph for a story. The well-read, well-rounded liberal-arts student has this advantage over the J-school graduate.

I am not against journalism schools. There are some fine ones, notably at Columbia University, the University of Missouri and Boston University. I just believe that a liberal-arts education provides better preparation for a career in journalism.

In my case, I had little choice in where I went to college. The University of Massachusetts at Amherst—just 36 miles from Gardner, my hometown—was the only school I could afford, and I felt fortunate to be able to go there. It offered only one course in journalism; I enrolled in it and liked it. The grade of 90 that I received further confirmed my choice of career field. The highlight of the course was an assignment to cover an address by poet Robert Frost at Amherst College, a couple of miles across town. Later in life, I was to meet the crusty, white-haired poet in person and obtain his autograph.

Journalism attracts thousands of students for much the reasons I chose to enter the field. According to the U.S. Department of Education, bachelor's degrees in journalism were conferred on 11,443 students in 1992–93. Women outnumbered men nearly 2 to 1. Competition for jobs in journalism is increasing sharply as newspapers and other news organizations "downsize," "rightsize" or "reconfigure" their staffs. As a result of this restructuring, 3,100 newsroom jobs—a little more than 5 percent of the journalistic work force—have been eliminated in the past six years.

12

Gardner

Radio played a big role in my life when I was a boy. There was no television in the 1930s. Radio provided entertainment as well as the news. Indeed, my earliest ambition was not to be a newsperson but to be a singer like Rudy Vallee whom we listened to regularly on the radio. We listened to afternoon soap operas, such as "One Man's Family," and to special events such as heavyweight boxer Joe Louis's fights against German fighter Max Schmeling. The world was edging close to global warfare that last year we lived in Hoosick Falls, and we all booed Schmeling roundly.

I vividly remember, too, how intently my parents listened to radio reports of the German bombing raids on Britain. When the radio reported the Luftwaffe had struck the bridge over the Firth of Forth on the Scottish east coast, they knew the war was on for them, even though U.S. entry into the war was two years off; that was getting too close to the homes they had left behind when they came to the United States.

My father received a promotion in his railroad job as a signal maintainer, and was transferred to Gardner in 1940. My parents took Jean, Frances and Gordon with them in our 1936 blue Oldsmobile—that's all they could fit in the car—and arranged for Margaret and me to follow by train.

Gardner was much larger than Brattleboro or Hoosick Falls. A busy industrial town with a population of about 18,000, it was known far and wide for the fine furniture that it produced—Heywood-Wakefield, S. Bent, Conant & Ball and Hedstrom's were names well known in the industry. So many chairs were made there that Gardner was called the "Chair City of the World."

Housing was hard to come by in Gardner so my parents rented a duplex in Otter River, a village of some 400 souls out in the country, five miles from Gardner. My father's drinking problem immediately got him into trouble with the Otter River police.

One night as he was returning home after drinking too much, a policeman stopped him and charged him with driving under the influence of alcohol. He lost his driver's license and, as a means of assuring reliable transportation to and from work, tried to teach my mother how to drive. The poor woman could never really get the hang of it, largely because he would harangue her whenever she made a mistake; she was greatly relieved when he got his license back. So were we children.

What I remember most about Otter River—besides beautiful, blonde Veronica Koziol in the fifth grade—were the summer months when the Polish family across the street took me and my sisters with them to pick blueberries. For the Hetniks and their cousins, the Sawickis, the money they got from picking blueberries was a necessity. Gabriel Hetnik, who had emigrated to America with his wife Johanna, was unable to work because of poor health. Their children, Henry, Irene, and Johnny, joined their mother every summer in picking blueberries to bring in extra money; they would bring me and my sisters along with them.

Early each morning, usually around 6 o'clock, Jean and I—and sometimes Frances—would climb into the Hetniks's pickup truck and head for Phillipston, 11 miles away, where there was an abundance of blueberries. The sweetest berries came from the low bushes; the tall bushes boasted larger ones but they were not as tasty. We would stay in the fields until 6 in the evening, picking berries under the hot sun, and swatting flies and other insects that came at us. Jean and I were usually exhausted by noon and wanted to go home but there was no way we could; we had to stay until the Hetniks were ready to leave and they often worked until early evening. I remember the experience for the sheer tiredness I felt. It was nice to get some spending money from the sale of the blueberries I had picked, but it was awfully hard work.

To get closer to his job, my father moved us to Gardner after a year and a half in Otter River. There again, he got into trouble with the law by driving under the influence of alcohol. After moves to two more rented houses, he bought a four-bedroom house for $4,300. The house at 101 South Main Street had more room than other houses we had lived in; even so, Gordon and I had to share a bed, as did Margaret and Frances. The place even had a backyard with a flower garden and a front lawn large enough to need mowing in the summer.

I loved flowers, and still do. In Brattleboro, my mother had a little garden near the sidewalk in front of our house where she planted nasturtiums, flowers I prefer above all others even to this day because of their happy, smiling faces.

She instilled this love of flowers in all of us by giving us each an old magazine, and sending us out to a nearby woods to collect as many different wild flowers as we could find, pressing them between the magazine's pages. The rarest of all was a jack-in-the pulpit. She made a contest of it: whichever child collected the most different flowers won a prize.

In Gardner, she planted day lilies, roses and marigolds. I helped her weed the garden, always feeling connected to something greater than myself. To earn money, I took care of a much larger garden at the home of Gardner's representative in the Massachusetts state legislature, Fred Blake.

13

Pearl Harbor

On the day the Japanese bombed Pearl Harbor—December 7, 1941—I was walking home from the First Baptist Church on East Broadway, where we children attended Sunday School. When I got home, the radio was blaring the news of the attack and President Roosevelt's announcement that the United States was at war.

On that "day of infamy," as FDR called it, I was just a couple of months past my 12th birthday. As no other event in the 70-plus years I have been on the planet, World War Two galvanized America into action and unified her people. We were unified because the stakes were clear and our focus undistorted: we saw our very survival as a nation hanging in the balance.

Unlike the Korean War, Vietnam and other military actions since then, Americans volunteered in droves to put on a uniform and fight for their country. My father, who was 44 years old at the time, sought to enlist in the Seabees, a construction battalion that built airstrips, roads and other infrastructure in the Pacific theater and elsewhere. He was turned away, however, because of his responsibilities to a large family. When the war ended, in August 1945, I was nearing my 16th birthday and so never had the opportunity to get in the fight. Instead, as a Boy Scout, I served as a junior air warden, making sure that neighbors blackened their windows during practice air raid alerts.

During the war, I delivered the morning *Worcester Telegram* to some 60 subscribers before school opened. It was hard work; the newspapers were heavy and the bag in which I carried them would cut into my shoulder; in the winter I froze and suffered lingering colds. As I walked

45

my three-mile route, I would read the paper's front page and keep up with the war news. Day after day, long troop convoys from Fort Devens would pass by on their way to the front. As with other Americans, it heartened me to read of allied victories and when the tide turned against us I was saddened by the loss of so many young men, some of them my neighbors.

Germany's surrender on May 7, 1945 was greeted with relief. We knew that the war was about to end and we'd return to normalcy. But news that the United States had dropped an atomic bomb on the Japanese city of Hiroshima, killing some 75,000 people, left us wondering about the world's future. I remember the day, August 6, for the eeriness the news created; people stopped each other in the streets, asking if they had ever heard of such a weapon. It was as if time had stood still. Few people could even grasp the meaning of an "atomic" bomb, its development had been so secret.

Shortly after Japan capitulated, the *U.S.S. Missouri*—the battleship on whose teak deck General Douglas MacArthur formally accepted Japan's surrender from Foreign Minister Mamoru Shigemitsu—anchored in Boston harbor and allowed visitors to board her. Just a teenager, I used my Boston & Maine railroad pass to get to Boston to see the historic vessel. How thrilled I was to be aboard the ship where World War Two ended. The momentousness of the occasion overwhelmed me; I felt part of history.

The newspaper delivery job that I had gave me a measure of economic freedom. It netted me enough money to buy my first suit and a three-piece bedroom suite. I was still wetting the bed but not as frequently. I was doing well in school, but felt guilt and shame because of the stuttering and bed-wetting. I had a tremendous inferiority complex.

When I entered high school, the bed-wetting ended and I didn't stutter as much. I made the honor list, belonged to several clubs, represented the school at Boys' State at the University of Massachusetts in Amherst, and managed the track team. I also found an outlet for my writing—the *Argus*, the high-school student quarterly magazine—and occasionally reported on high-school athletic events for *The Gardner News,* the local daily newspaper.

After school, I worked at WHOB, the Gardner radio station, putting together newscasts from wireless reports for station announcers to read. The station's offices were located in the Colonial Hotel. I remember showing up for work one day only to learn that one of the announcers was no longer there. It turned out that announcer Ben Hubley was an army deserter, and that the authorities had finally caught up with him and taken him into custody. It saddened me because he seemed like such a nice guy.

At graduation, my classmates voted me "Most Dependable." The class yearbook had this comment next to my picture: "Few things are impossible to diligence and skill." Quite a billing to live up to. I also was awarded a $100 scholarship, which in 1947 was a lot of money.

Academically, I ranked 11th in a graduating class of 169. The courses that prepared me most for a career in journalism were English, Latin and typewriting. An estimated 50 percent of the English language derives from Latin, and the touch-typing system I learned and use to this day is far superior to the hunt-and-peck method.

How different high school was half a century ago. When I heard about the tragic school shootings in Jonesboro, Arkansas; Paducah, Kentucky; Littleton, Colorado, and Santee, California, I could not help but contrast student behavior then with student behavior today. The worst incident in my four years at Gardner High School involved a student caught smoking a cigarette in the boys' room.

14

Working on the Railroad

No one in my immediate family had ever gone to college. Margaret, Frances and Jean, like most young women of their generation, were expected to take a job after high-school graduation, marry and raise a family, which my three sisters did. For the rest of her life, Frances was embittered by the lack of opportunity to go on to college.

My brother Gordon earned a bachelor's degree from the University of Wyoming while serving in the Air Force.

Thanks in part to my mother's encouragement, I made it. I had the grades, and I had the money; I had been saving throughout high school.

Because of his employment with the Boston & Maine, my father was able to get me a summer job on the railroad. For five straight summers, I sweated and toiled digging ditches to lay cable for railroad signal crossings. My mother, who saw herself as my "treasurer," would put away my union wage-scale earnings so that when I entered the University of Massachusetts, I had enough to cover first-year expenses.

It may be of interest to note that, in 1947, the year I entered the university, tuition was $50 a semester for Massachusetts residents, or $100 for the academic year. Total enrollment then was about 3,600 students; today, enrollment is approximately 26,000 and the university is frequently referred to as "Zoomass" because of the crowded campus.

While the railroad job was the main source of my earnings in college I supplemented my income by writing publicity articles for the university's athletics department, reporting campus news activities for the old

Boston Post and enrolling in the Air Force Reserve Officers' Training Course (ROTC).

ROTC cadets received $22 a semester; we also got a complete uniform which we were allowed to wear to classes, thus reducing our clothing expenses; we'd wear the jacket, gloves, shirts and sweaters even when we weren't attending military courses.

15

My First Drink

Though I did not recognize its significance until much later in life, I had my first alcoholic drink at UMass. At the end of classes my senior year, the fraternity I belonged to—Lambda Chi Alpha—celebrated the event with a beer bust in the chapter's party room, the "Cave."

For whatever reason, perhaps the uncertainty of going into military service during wartime, I chug-a-lugged a few drinks and felt quite relaxed and uninhibited. Fraternity brother Marty Flynn referred to me the next day as "Laughing Boy." It was the start of a drinking career that would not end for 18 years; the drinking hurt not only my career but also kept me from forming any lasting relationship with a woman.

As I reflect upon the episode, I think my drinking resulted from an admixture of fear, poor self-esteem, guilt, shame, and loneliness.

From my first year at the university through graduation, I wrote for the *Collegian*, the university newspaper. Most of what I wrote were features, though I also covered breaking news events. At graduation, the university honored me with an award for my activities with the publication. Back then, in the Forties and Fifties, the *Collegian* was a weekly paper staffed sporadically by students as they were able to fit reporting assignments into their class schedule; none of us was paid. Today, the *Collegian* is an award-winning daily newspaper whose top editors are well paid.

Betty Krieger, the *Collegian* editor and a year ahead of me, liked to say, "journalism is abbreviated history and the *Collegian is* abbreviated journalism." Krieger later joined the staff of the *Worcester Telegram and Gazette* as did I later in my career.

Serving as the campus correspondent was a tough way to earn a dollar, but every little bit helped. More important, the experience was priceless for someone choosing journalism as a career. The newspaper paid 30 cents an inch for stories it printed, $1 for a one-column photo and $2 for a photo measuring two columns or larger.

The *Post's* way of assigning me to cover an event was to send me a Western Union telegram; I lacked the funds to have a telephone of my own. The city desk might wire, as they did, for example, "Gov dedicates new lab 300." Translation: "Send us a 300-word story on the governor's dedication of a new laboratory at the university." And 300 words—no more, no less—is what they wanted.

My first "byline" in a major newspaper was in the *Post*. I was thrilled. I had realized the dream I had nourished 10 years earlier when the Linotype operator at the Hoosick Falls newspaper set my name in lead. There it was, "By Jim Shevis," in boldface type above the article headed, "Tufts Wins, 27–7 Over U. of Mass."

The article appeared on page 33 of the *Post's* November 13, 1950 sports section." The story recounted the season's finale for the UMass football team, which had suffered its fourth straight loss.

The article measured 18 inches long. At the *Post's* going rate of 30 cents an inch for a story that made its way into print, I was paid $5.40. But much more than the modest compensation, the boost in self-confidence and self-esteem it gave me was incalculable.

16

The Air Force

I didn't jump straight into professional journalism from college, however. In 1951, the year I graduated from the University of Massachusetts, there was a war going on in Korea that involved the United States. It was called a United Nations "police action." I and other newly commissioned ROTC officers had orders to report for active duty three months before we graduated.

During the war, I served 21 months in the Air Force, half of that time in California, the other half in Japan. After honorable separation from the Air Force in 1953, I spent the next seven years in career fields directly or indirectly related to journalism. I was an advertising copywriter for General Electric at its huge Schenectady, New York plant; taught high-school English in the mill town of Barre, Massachusetts, and did a stint with the federal government at Cape Canaveral, Florida. When I finally answered my true calling—journalism—I was 31 years old.

I never thought of those years after leaving the Air Force as wasted years. The time I spent writing copy touting G.E. locomotives and distribution transformers, or teaching Barre High School students English all yielded benefits in ways hard to explain. It was as if I were stoking up experiences to draw upon in my future career as a journalist.

As graduation neared, I found myself peering into an uncertain future. The United States was mired in the war in Korea and I might be sent there. As a newly minted Air Force officer, I had orders in my hand to report to Wright-Patterson Air Force Base in Dayton, Ohio for active duty. After four years in a relatively sheltered environment, I pondered: where do I go from here with the rest of my life?

Early in May, just days before formal graduation exercises, I wandered into the university's Goodell Library and, while searching through the stacks for I know not what, stumbled upon Samuel Johnson's 18th-century novel, *History of Rasselas, Prince of Abyssinia*, a book that has caused me to think deeply about life ever since. The novel is about a young man's quandary over what to do with his life—making choices.

According to the story line, Rasselas has grown up in The Happy Valley with everything one could ask for, but he is not happy; he escapes in order to find what to do with his life. In the end, after much wandering and soul searching, he concludes—like the Prodigal Son—that life back home in the valley wasn't that bad after all.

Through the fictional characters, Dr. Johnson muses on the meaning of life and what man was put on Earth to do. The work is sprinkled with memorable snippets of wisdom. One character says, for instance, "Nothing will ever be attempted, if all possible objections must be first overcome"—the perfect response to those who would procrastinate.

Rasselas's journey is much like that of others, including mine. I found it easy to identify with him. We are restless, it seems, even when we appear to have everything. I have thought of the Abyssinian prince over the years, wondering whether I will ever be satisfied with my lot.

For the next two years anyway, I knew where I was going. I was going on active duty with the Air Force. I'm glad I enrolled in Air Force ROTC, and not Army ROTC, at UMass. Some of those who chose the Army were sent to Korea and never came home.

The Korean War was a byproduct of the long Cold War between the Communist and non-Communist systems following World War Two. It resulted from a so-called "police action" undertaken by the United Nations to stem Communist aggression on the Korean peninsula. No formal declaration of war was made, however.

Years later, when my son asked me, "Dad, what did you do in the (Korean) war," I told him, jokingly, but truthfully: "I fought the Battles of San Francisco and Tokyo." Which is to say that, rather than being where there was enemy fire, I was assigned to Air Force installations near those two cities where I was safe from bodily harm.

All things considered, I had an easy time of it. On weekends, a buddy and I frequently drove the 90 miles to San Francisco from McClellan Air Force Base in Sacramento in hopes of meeting women. In Japan, where I was stationed at Johnson Air Force Base northwest of Tokyo, I rode the Japanese railway into Tokyo to see the sights.

After initial processing at Wright-Patterson Air Force Base in Dayton, Ohio, I and several other ROTC officers were transferred to McClellan, a really posh facility. There, I was assigned to the base public information office because of my journalistic activities at UMass. Besides writing press releases about airmen for their hometown newspapers, I served as liaison between McClellan and the California State Fair in Sacramento. But my most memorable experience while stationed at McClellan occurred off base in mid-January 1952.

17

Drama at Donner Pass

One evening, while I was having dinner at the officers' club, a call came over the public-address system for a volunteer to assist in the rescue of 226 passengers and crew trapped aboard the City *of San Francisco,* the Southern Pacific Railroad's crack streamliner. The call smacked of adventure, and so I volunteered.

On Sunday, January 13, in a raging blizzard, the 15-car train rammed into a deep snowslide high in the Sierra Nevada mountains at Donner Pass. When engineers threw the train into reverse to escape the avalanche, its wheels slipped on the icy tracks.

No one panicked. After all, the train was more powerful and better equipped than any on the line. No one really expected to be there very long. But the situation turned serious when a rotary snowplow sent to extricate the train experienced equipment failure and became stranded too.

Winters at Donner Pass are invariably brutal, and this winter had been particularly bad. Nearly 13 feet of snow had fallen when the train became snowbound. Wind estimated at 80 and 90 miles an hour blew sheets of snow down the canyon and onto the tracks.

A century earlier, Donner Pass gained notoriety when a party of American migrants was trapped by similar heavy snows there. The group suffered enormous hardships and ultimately resorted to cannibalism to survive. Now the ancient pass threatened another Donner party.

Boarding an eastbound rescue train in Sacramento, I took charge of half a dozen enlisted men who had also volunteered for the rescue mission. Other trains sought to reach the streamliner from Reno. Ours finally broke through 12-foot snowdrifts to come within four and a half-miles of the marooned train. Highway crews then cleared a road paralleling the tracks, enabling passengers to walk to safety.

Strong winds and heavy snows hampered the rescue operation. The storm broke three days after the train became stranded, allowing rescue parties to punch their way through to the train; all aboard the streamliner survived the ordeal.

What I remember most about the rescue effort was the bitter cold and exhaustion we experienced. Temperatures were well below freezing; none of us slept much. Photos of me and the men show us looking gaunt and weary.

I remember reports, too, of a crisis brought on by a drug-addicted passenger who went berserk when he could not get his next fix. Rescuers locked him in his compartment until the train returned to Sacramento.

18

Assignment: Japan

As the Korean War heated up, my days at McClellan were numbered and I was reassigned to the Far East. It was just as well, for my drinking had got me onto some slippery slopes. Officers' clubs throughout the military are notorious for their alcohol-related events. Happy hours, in which drinks are either free or very cheap, are commonplace at officers' clubs even today. I spent too many hours drinking at the officers' club but that did not make me happy. Drinking for me was a way of feeling more confident about myself. Even though I had those shiny lieutenant's bars on my shoulders, I did not feel comfortable as an officer. When some grizzled, old master sergeant saluted me, I often felt guilty. What did I know about being an officer? All of this, I learned many years later, is characteristic of an adult child of an alcoholic.

After a two-week sail across the Pacific, the troop ship carrying me and hundreds of other Americans arrived in Yokohama. Before debarking, we were warned to take precautions in any sexual relations we might get involved in. "Some of these women have diseases there's no name for," we were told. That didn't stop many GI's from exploring native haunts. I myself was too scared to try my luck.

Processing in Nagoya took a couple of days before I was assigned, in May 1952, to Johnson Air Base near Tokyo as adjutant of the 35th Fighter-Interceptor Group. An adjutant is someone who helps the unit commander with administrative work, especially correspondence—a "paper-pusher," if you will.

My secondary duty was that of a public information officer. I also sat on court-martial boards and accident-investigation panels.

A former Japanese military installation, Johnson Air Base had a storied past. The Americans took it over in January 1946, four months after Japan surrendered. One of the first things I saw in the morning when I left my BOQ (bachelor officers' quarters) for work was beautiful, snow-capped Mount Fuji, at 12,389 feet, Japan's highest mountain. As the country's sacred mountain, Fujiyama—a two-hour drive from Tokyo—is visited annually by thousands of Japanese.

The base was named in honor of Lieutenant Gerald R. Johnson, a Pacific theater flying ace in World War Two. Johnson shot down 22 Japanese airplanes before his plane crashed in Japan in 1946, killing him.

During World War Two, when the Japanese held it, the base was known as the Toyooka Flying Cadet School. It was there that Japanese kamikaze pilots were trained to fly suicidal missions on a target, many of them against American warships. It was also the place where the Japanese reportedly beheaded American prisoners. After the war, Johnson became part of the Japan Air Defense Force (JADF). JADF's mission was to defend Honshu, Japan's main island, from any aggressor.

Johnson was regarded as a good duty assignment. Except for its potholed, axle-breaking roads, the base had all the amenities of life, including an 18-hole golf course, two swimming pools, a movie theater, a library and a well-stocked commissary. High-ranking officers were allowed to bring their wives and children there. Tokyo's glittering Ginza district was only 45 minutes away by rail.

I liked the base, and I liked my assignment as adjutant. As adjutant, I came to know many of the pilots who flew the group's planes—the propeller-driven F-51s and the F-80 and F-94 jets. I'd like to have been a pilot myself, but an astigmatism kept me from flight training.

Most of the pilots were about my age, 22 or 23, and I lived their adventures vicariously. They were a fun-loving group, though the F-94 crews often seemed tense—and with good reason. They flew nighttime missions to Korea in all kinds of weather, and returned with some scary stories. The F-51 and F-80 pilots stayed in Japan, training and on alert status.

In 1952, when he was campaigning for the American presidency, Dwight Eisenhower pledged, "I will go to Korea" to bring the stalemated war to an end, a promise he carried out. Pilots of the 35th Fighter-Interceptor Group flew escort for the candidate's plane in a secret mission called "Operation Extra Whisky."

What I learned about pilots was their love of adventure and the feeling of freedom they experienced when they're off in the wild blue yonder. If they feel they can get away with it, too, they'll go for the big "rush" that comes from "hot-dogging"—that is, flying at tree-top level, buzzing a friend's house, and showing off in general.

One F-94 backseater I knew—a married first lieutenant from New Jersey—developed a deep fear of flying and wanted reassignment. Once or twice a week, he came to my office and pored over Air Force regulations in search of a way home. I don't know whether he ever found it. He was still at Johnson when I returned to the United States in February 1953.

One pilot I knew made it back, but not the way he wanted it. While flying an F-51 on a training mission in bad weather, he developed vertigo—spatial disorientation—and flew the plane into a mountainside. If he had trusted his instruments instead of his intuition he wouldn't have "bought the farm," flyers' slang for a fatal crash.

19

Double Jet Ace

But there were other pilots who thrived living on the edge and flew in the face of danger, enjoying every minute of it. First Lieutenant Harold E. Fischer, a farm boy from Swea City, Iowa, was one of them.

Two things about Fischer struck me the day we met in late 1952. Though our meeting was brief, I remember his lanky, carefree gait and loose, easy-going manner. The other feature that stands out in my memory was his eyes, piercing and steel-like. He seemed somehow different from other fighter pilots I had met.

He had wandered into my office, looking for the personnel office. I gave him directions and never saw him again until 40 years later when I was researching this book. But the memory of this daring flyer remained with me over the years as much for his calm and cool demeanor as for his exploits during the war.

Fischer had already flown 105 ground-support missions in F-80 jets in Korea. What he wanted to do next was to fly the swifter, more versatile F-86 Sabrejet in aerial combat. He wanted to become an ace, defined as a pilot who has shot down five or more enemy planes.

In the book, *Top Guns*, by Joe Foss and Matthew Brennan (Pocket Books, New York, 1991), a collection of stories by American fighter aces, Fischer wrote: "My talks with jet aces began to excite me. One of the aces told me that experienced pilots were needed and, with diligence, I could become an ace."

The Air Force gave him his chance, and granted him another tour in Korea where he was assigned to the 51st Fighter-Interceptor Wing at Suwon. He checked out in the highly maneuverable F-86—a plane that reminded me of a swallow—and was soon shooting Russian-built MiG fighters out of the sky.

The 27-year-old flyer said he preferred what he called "Kentucky windage"—leading MiGs like ducks—to the Air Force's famed radar gunsight.

Fischer shot down 10 Communist MiGs in his 66 combat missions, qualifying him as a double jet ace. But his luck ran out on April 7, 1953 when he was forced to bail out of his damaged jet during a dogfight with a MiG. He was captured in Manchuria, and spent over two years as a prisoner of the Chinese communists.

Fischer stayed in the Air Force after his release from Communist prison camps. In Vietnam, he flew Huey helicopters and served as an adviser to the South Vietnamese.

In 1993, forty years after he was shot down, I flew out to Las Vegas, where Fischer lived in a retirement community, to interview him. We chatted amiably for about three hours but could not agree on conditions for a formal interview. The result was that I decided not to pursue the matter.

Fischer retired from the Air Force in 1979 as a full colonel, and has kept busy with other interests since then. "Don't ever retire," he admonished me. "You'll be busier than ever." These days he travels, attends fighter-ace reunions, and is "into" cars, airplanes and computers.

20

What Else is Out There?

I liked the Air Force and the camaraderie I enjoyed with the young fighter pilots I had come to know at Johnson. I had been promoted from second to first lieutenant and had done some traveling in Japan. But when my 21-month tour-of-duty contract with the Air Force neared completion, I elected to leave the military. I wanted to see what else was out there—something I have done several times in my life. If I had stayed in the Air Force for 20 years or so, I'd probably have made full colonel. But one never knows about such things.

I was released from active duty and separated from the Air Force at Otis Air Force Base in Falmouth, Massachusetts on March 12, 1953. At that time, I was awarded the Korean Service Medal, with one battle star, and the United Nations Service Medal. (The F-94 sorties into North Korea made me eligible for the battle star by association.)

A half-century later, I received a Certificate of Recognition from Defense Secretary William S. Cohen for my participation in winning the Cold War. The certificate read: "For your service during the period of the Cold War (2 September 1945 to 26 December 1991) in promoting peace and stability for this Nation, the people of this Nation are forever grateful."

The Cold War is said to have started with Japan's formal surrender during World War Two, and ended with the breakup of the Soviet Union.

It was a standard certificate for which hundreds of thousands of Americans were eligible. All they needed to do was apply, as I did, with proof that they had served during the Cold War period. The Army, the executive agent for the program, had printed one million certificates as of April 1999.

It was a nice gesture of the government, but I must confess I never thought of myself as a Cold War warrior. A Korean War veteran, yes—even if the only battles I fought were the Battles of San Francisco and Tokyo. But I had to ponder my part in the superpower confrontation between the United States and the Soviet Union. It never occurred to me that I had played a role in the conflict.

I can look back now and remember when the Cold War threatened to turn hot, however. That was during the 1962 Cuban missile crisis when many Americans, including myself, thought the United States and the Soviet Union were on the brink of nuclear war. Believing that a global conflagration was imminent, I looked into the possibility of reentering the Air Force. The crisis passed, however, and, breathing a sigh of relief, I pursued my career in journalism instead.

The Cold War kept much of the world on tenterhooks for years, and was not without its casualties. More than 33,000 U.S. service members died in the Korean War and over 55,000 Americans died in Vietnam. America's allies also sustained casualties while its opponents suffered even greater losses.

For all the Americans who never returned from Korea and Vietnam, it would have been an even nicer gesture if the government had made its Cold War certificates available to their families.

When I left the Air Force, I wasn't sure what I would do with my life, though I had a glimmer of an idea. At 23 years old, I wanted to see more of the world. Now that I had seen a bit of the Orient, I thought travel and study in Europe would give me a nice launching pad into a career in international affairs.

The Institute of International Relations in New York accepted me for study in the United Kingdom right away, but indecisiveness on my part led me to heed my mother's advice to stay home, find a job and settle down. I quickly found a job as advertising manager for Goodnow Pearson's in Gardner, the largest department store in northern Worcester County. But it didn't seem to match my ideas of what to do with my life. I felt much like Rasselas, who wandered for years in an attempt to find the path of life.

I had heard that the best journalism school in the United States was at the University of Missouri, and so I applied for admission there and was accepted as a graduate student. I quit my job at Goodnow's, and boarded a train for Missouri. In what I can only say was a further sign of indecisiveness—psychologists call it "approach avoidance," i.e., reaching a decision, then backing off from it—I got as far as St. Louis before I changed my mind and returned to Gardner.

I soon found an excellent opportunity as a trainee in the General Electric Company's advertising and sales promotion program in Schenectady, New York.

My first assignment was with G.E.'s employee and plant communications department, interacting with the community and singing paeans of praise in behalf of the company's good-neighbor policy.

It was a time in the Cold War when the Red scare in America produced what came to be known as McCarthyism—Wisconsin Senator Joseph McCarthy's relentless campaign against alleged communists in the government. The Republican senator also investigated alleged Communist Party activity among union workers at G.E.'s Schenectady plant, holding hearings in nearby Albany.

Recognizing the historical importance of the event, I went to Albany on my own time and attended the second of two consecutive hearings, this one on February 19, 1954. I was simply an observer, but found myself itching to cover the event as a news reporter. The hearings produced nothing of substance, except a further display of McCarthy's witch-hunt tactics.

My second training assignment in Schenectady was with G.E.'s advertising and sales promotion department where I wrote ads for General Electric locomotives that appeared in *Fortune* and *Business Week* magazines. During this period of time, I became infatuated with a young woman down the hall from my office. It was a case of unrequited love, which was bad enough, but I made matters worse by turning to alcohol to ease the pain. My work suffered as a result, and I was transferred to G.E.'s power transformer department in Pittsfield, Massachusetts in the belief that a change of scenery might help me get over my personal problems.

Suffice to say, the problems lingered even after I began counseling. I'd like to say that I never experienced such emotional turmoil again, but the truth is that years later I did. However, as a line in a song by Scottish singer Jean Ritchie has it, "sad experience teaches me," and the earlier experience helped me to better handle the new hurt.

After three years of writing high-profile G.E. ads for large-circulation magazines, I left the company to try my hand at teaching.

With only a summer's session at the Harvard-Newton teaching program behind me, I took on the task of teaching freshman and senior English at Barre High School in Barre, Massachusetts. I failed miserably. I was unable to handle classroom discipline. Without adequate preparation, I was a sitting duck for some smart-aleck students whom I let get the best of me. Halfway through the school year, Principal Roy Dawson asked me to leave.

To lick my wounds, I went to Florida where I accepted an invitation from my sister Jean and her husband Reo Hill to stay with them while I sorted things out. Reo, who was my age, was an air-traffic controller at Patrick Air Force Base near Cape Canaveral. He had been in the Air Force for years. As I was to discover, he was an alcoholic. Nonetheless, he and Jean and their three young daughters made me feel part of their family, which helped immensely in my recovery. A load seemed to lift from my shoulders; I lightened up and began to take life less seriously. After a year with the Hills, I returned to Gardner and found what I have always thought to be my true calling—journalism.

21

$60-a-Week Reporter

What spurred me into journalism were the 1960 Kennedy-Nixon presidential debates, the first of which I listened to on my car radio as I drove north to Gardner. I was caught up by Kennedy's optimism, which stirred me to believe that somehow, somewhere, there was something better awaiting me than a humdrum life in blue-collar Gardner.

Staying at my parents' home, I found a job in a box factory doing piecework—hardly the glamorous calling I had hoped for. No matter. It didn't last long. The boss fired me the first week because he thought I wasn't keeping up with the work pace.

The baseball World Series was in progress, and the fall foliage colors were at their peak. Central Massachusetts was never so beautiful. What more could one ask for? Without a job, I yet felt all would work out well.

In what Carl Jung might call "synchronicity," I walked into the Gardner office of the *Worcester Telegram* & *Gazette* one day and inquired about employment. Julian Grow, the bureau chief, said it just so happened that the newspaper was looking for a staff reporter in Gardner. He arranged an interview with Executive Editor Leslie Moore in Worcester, who hired me as a $60-a-week reporter.

It was the start of a 35-year career in journalism and a life of excitement—even glamour at times.

22

The Worcester Telegram &
Gazette

I n journalism, there is what's called "hard news" and there is "soft news." Hard news is a factual, objective account of an event such as a murder, a city council meeting or a fire. Soft news can be a feature story, an editorial, a column or a news analysis.

At the *Telegram & Gazette*, and throughout my career, I wrote both hard news and soft news, but I preferred the latter. A hard-news story and a feature have quite different structures. The structure of a hard-news story resembles an inverted pyramid, with the most important information provided in the lead paragraph and less important information in succeeding paragraphs.

Hard-news writing is formula writing that a rookie reporter can pick up in a week or so. Features also have a structure but require more thought and creativity. I preferred feature-writing because it allowed me to express my own style. I learned early in the game, too, that I was more apt to get a byline on a feature than on a run-of-the-mill hard-news story. Having my name on a published article was a matter of no small importance to me. It's one of the great satisfactions for a print reporter. It's a morale booster.

About a year after I joined the *Telegram & Gazette*—the *Telegram* was the morning paper, the *Gazette* the afternoon paper—I learned that one of the McGuire Sisters—a popular singing trio at the time—spent her summers at a lake in New Hampshire just over the Massachusetts line. The McGuire Sisters were a close-harmony pop trio in the '50s and '60s whose style has since disappeared; but they were big time and nationally known in the 1960s.

I figured that a Chris McGuire feature would make good, light reading for *Telegram and Gazette* readers. Because her summer camp was located outside the newspaper's circulation area, I first had to convince the news desk in Worcester that an article about the singer was worth the space. I succeeded in doing this by convincing the desk that an article with a New Hampshire dateline might lead to expanded circulation.

The interview went well and at the end of it Chris inscribed the following on a black-and-white photo of the trio:

> "To Jim
> "Enjoyed the interview.
> "Lots and Lots of Luck.
>   "Chris McGuire"

23

Robert Frost

Ten days after the McGuire article appeared in the *Telegram*, I had the good fortune to attend the Bread Loaf Writers' Conference at Middlebury College in Vermont. Held annually the last two weeks in August, the conference brings together writers of every shade of talent and non-talent and teachers of writing who care about the writing craft.

The oldest and most respected of its kind in the country, the conference has served as the model for scores of other writers' conferences that have sprung up in the United States and abroad. Set in the Green Mountains of Vermont, the conference takes its name from a nearby mountain that resembles a loaf of bread. The poet Robert Frost was a major force in creating Bread Loaf and was closely associated with it until his death in 1963.

Bread Loaf in 1961 was a magical place. Its pastoral quiet and beauty, its unhurried pace, good talk, and companionship combined to create an atmosphere in which conference members could learn more about writing.

I attribute whatever success I have had as a writer and reporter in part to my two-week stay at Bread Loaf and to the time I spent with United Press International. Both experiences taught me to write to be understood, to choose the Anglo-Saxon word over a Latin or Greek derivative, to write with order, style and economy of words.

Frost was at Bread Loaf the summer I was there. We met quite by chance. The door to his second-floor office in the Bread Loaf Inn was ajar one morning and I saw him standing there, his hair tousled and looking as if he were trying to figure out what his next move would be. I said hello, and we struck up a conversation. I mustered the courage to ask for his autograph, something I had rarely asked anyone for; it would not be the last time, however. Frost willingly scrawled his name on the frontispiece of John F. Kennedy's *Profiles in Courage,* a paperback book which I had brought with me to read:

"Robert Frost
"An admirer
"1961"

Frost was a special lecturer at Bread Loaf that summer. In an August 29 address to conference members, he spoke of poetry and the meaning of poetry. I kept notes on some of what he said in that afternoon seminar.

"You don't have to know how to spell to write poetry. You don't have to know how to punctuate at all," he said. "You have to know what an idea is. You've got to know the difference between an idea that will do in prose and one that will do in poetry.

"Poetry is not poetry unless it is passionate, emotional," he said—a remark reminiscent of William Wordsworth's comment: "Poetry is the spontaneous overflow of powerful feelings; it takes its origin from emotion recollected in tranquility."

Frost had no use for poets and poetry whose meaning was obscure or indecipherable. When someone asked him, "What do you do with a poem you can't understand?" he said, disdainfully: "What do you do with a fool?" The implication was you don't waste your time with either poem or fool.

Besides Frost, the Bread Loaf staff included Howard Nemerov, who went on to win the Pulitzer Prize for poetry in 1978; freelance writer Bernard Asbell *(When FDR Died);* novelist Theodore Morrison; poet Dudley Fitts, and short-story writer William Hazlett Upson. Asbell had been assigned to evaluate samples of my articles since he dealt in non-fiction.

Heading this group of distinguished writers was the poet and critic, John Ciardi. Ciardi had been a lecturer at Bread Loaf since 1947 and served as its director from 1955–1972. An immensely gifted man, Ciardi was poetry editor for *Saturday Review* magazine from 1956–1972, translator of Dante's *Inferno* in 1954, and a popular writer of children's poetry.

"Poetry is to be experienced, not paraphrased or read for meaning," Ciardi said in a 1961 Bread Loaf lecture. "It's more important to experience a poem than to judge it."

By now, I was moved to add the signatures of Ciardi, Upson and Asbell to my meager collection of autographs—Ciardi's on the cover of the June 3, 1961 *Saturday Review* carrying his article, *How to Read Dante.*

24

My First Autograph

*"I stopped believing in Santa Claus when I was
six. Mother took me to see him in a
department store, and he asked me
for my autograph."*

—— Shirley Temple

The first autograph that I acquired was that of Maurice J. Tobin. I
still have it 50 years later, the notepaper on which it was written
only slightly brown with age.

Maurice Tobin never attained the status of a household name,
although he was well known and highly regarded in his home state of
Massachusetts and in Washington. But in 1946, when he was governor
of Massachusetts, this quintessential Boston politician—hair slicked
back, a ready smile, and a voice of dulcet tones—had all of us Boys
State delegates hanging on his every word.

We were a captive audience that summer, chosen by our high-
school teachers and administrators across the state to attend the good-
government workshop at Massachusetts State College (later renamed
the University of Massachusetts) in Amherst. Our selection to the
American Legion-sponsored event was considered an honor.

World War Two had ended less than a year earlier. Thoroughly
imbued with the righteousness of America's role in that long, drawn-
out conflict, we 16- and 17-year-olds responded to Tobin's praise of
the American way of life with whistling and handclapping.

In my sheltered lifetime, I had not until then met such a high-ranking official—in effect, a celebrity—nor one who spoke so movingly. So moved was I that after he finished speaking I rushed up to him and asked for his autograph. He leaned over the podium and scribbled his name on a piece of paper I had given him.

Tobin was defeated in his bid for reelection four months later, but that was not the end of his political career. He went on to become U.S. Secretary of Labor in the Truman administration. When Tobin died in 1953 at the age of 52, President Truman and a future U.S. President—then-Senator John F. Kennedy—were among the mourners attending his funeral service.

I thought to myself at the time, how lucky I was to have obtained the autograph of one so exalted.

Over the years, I managed to acquire nearly 100 autographs of celebrities and newsmakers—most of them in my capacity as a journalist. While meeting such people is in itself not uncommon, what *is* uncommon is the range of backgrounds and forums within which the people I met existed and spread their messages.

Collecting autographs was never an overarching interest with me. I have been too busy reporting the news to devote much time to the activity. Rather, I think it derived in part from an innate predisposition toward acquiring "things." I'm not unique in this respect; other people collect things, too: earrings, buttons, pennants, dolls, hats, shoes, compact discs—even boyfriends and girlfriends, husbands and wives.

I believe that we all have the collecting instinct. Just as squirrels, bears, and other animals collect and store food to tide them over the winter, men and women collect things. Look at the homeless people in our big cities: they fill their grocery carts with all manner of things. People are simply acquisitive by nature.

When I was a teenager, I collected matchbook covers—not for their monetary worth but just to collect them. As an adult, I have collected postage stamps, neckties, and books among other "things." I recall collecting and numbering the few books that I owned when I was in the fifth grade; today, I have a library of over 1,000 volumes—a collection that would be larger if I did not weed them out from time to time.

Genetic or otherwise, my son Andy seems to have inherited the same predisposition. Andy began collecting baseball cards as a six-year-old Little Leaguer; by the time he was 12, he had 20,000. Like serious autograph collectors, Andy bought, sold, and traded them; he still has thousands stashed away in a bedroom closet.

The word "autograph" derives from the Greek word "autographs," meaning "something written in one's own hand." It is a person's signature on a photograph, a letter, a document, and a book—even a piece of scrap paper. Some of the autographs in my collection are on business cards, postcards, notepad paper, books and magazines.

Autograph collecting can be traced to ancient times when people wrote on baked hard tablets, but for all practical purposes autograph collecting did not begin until the advent of paper some 2,000 years ago. When printing developed in Europe in the 15th century, autograph collecting became widespread.

Today, there are thousands of individual autograph collectors all over the world. Institutions such as the U.S. Library of Congress, the British Museum, and the Vatican Library in Rome also collect and display signatures of famous people.

Some collectors specialize, seeking only the signatures of movie stars, television personalities or sports figures. Others, like myself, generalize and have autographs from people in a variety of fields.

While most collectors seek signatures only, others collect only autographed letters or documents of famous people. Such collectors may be individuals or institutions such as libraries or museums.

Most people acquire a few prized autographs in their lifetime. My wife Carol obtained Israeli Prime Minister Golda Meir's signature on a $2 bill. She also got the autograph of folksinger Burl Ives, her distant relative.

In 1995, the National Archives in Washington displayed a priceless collection of letters and documents titled "American Originals." The exhibit included 26 original documents handwritten or signed by famous Americans.

Among the items were President Nixon's 1974 resignation letter; Robert E. Lee's oath reaffirming his loyalty to the U.S. Constitution after surrendering his troops at the end of the Civil War; a petition for universal suffrage signed by Susan B. Anthony, Elizabeth Cady Stone, and Lucy Stanton in 1866; an 1889 letter signed by abolitionist Frederick Douglass accepting his appointment as U.S. envoy to Haiti, and a 1936 letter from famed aviator Amelia Earhart to President Roosevelt seeking government assistance in her ill-starred Pacific flight.

25

On Collecting Autographs

The law of supply and demand generally determines the value of an autograph: the fewer of the item, the greater the price. Other factors include the signer's identity, the autograph's authenticity, and the age and condition of the material. If the item is a letter or document, its contents are another factor in determining price.

There are a number of magazines, books, and newsletters that list selling prices of autographs. For instance, *Autograph* magazine, a leading publication in the field, said in its March 1996 issue that a signed Joe Louis photo was selling for $350–$650, "depending on the size and how nice it is."

When Andy and I were in Cooperstown, New York, a few years ago, a baseball signed by the late Mickey Mantle carried a $28,000 price tag at the Yankee slugger's outlet there.

Curious to know how much my *Profiles in Courage* paperback was worth, I called a dealer in LaJolla, California who had placed an ad in *Autograph* wanting to buy autographs. "I'd say around $1,000, without seeing it," he said. That was in December 1995.

I think it's worth more. How often are the signatures of John F. Kennedy, Robert Frost, and Marian Anderson found on the same page? The California dealer had an answer.

While agreeing that it was unique to have the three signatures on one page in a book written by the 35th American president, the dealer said the book would be worth more if JFK's signature were the only one on it.

"That's what collectors want," he said. "It's like baseball cards: Babe Ruth's signature alone on his card would be worth more than if other names were on it also."

I admired the dealer's candor, however; he said my book probably has "greater sentimental value" than monetary value. He's right. I don't intend to sell it.

What's the highest price ever paid for a single, signed autographed letter?

According to the *Guinness Book of Records*, the top figure was $748,000 for a letter written by Abraham Lincoln defending his Emancipation Proclamation. The letter was sold at Christie's in New York City on December 5, 1991 to Profiles in History of Beverly Hills, California.

Collecting autographs is a hobby for some and a business for others. For me, it's neither really. Rather, it's a sometimes thing generally motivated by a desire simply to have something to remember the person by. For the most part, I have sought the signatures only of people whom I admire and respect.

There are many ways of obtaining autographs. One, of course, is to go up to the person and ask for the autograph as I did with President Kennedy, poet Robert Frost, and singer Marian Anderson. Another is to request the autograph by mail, but this will not ensure that you will get an authentic autograph—or even a response, for that matter.

I once wrote Willy Mays, the star San Francisco Giants outfielder, for an autograph for my Little League son. Mays had retired from baseball, and was serving as a host at an Atlantic City casino at the time. I never got a reply.

Many famous people have their secretaries sign their name to keep up with fan mail and autograph requests. Or they'll use a mechanical device called an auto-pen that can sign up to 3,000 signatures in eight hours.

For example, U.S. Senator Charles E. Grassley (Republican-Iowa) uses an auto-pen. I know this because the signature on the photo and cover letter that his office sent me were identical, and both are different from the signature he wrote in my presence when we lunched together at the Senators' Dining Room in the Capitol.

Collectors may also buy autographs at auctions or from dealers. Again, the authenticity of autographs obtained in this manner may be questionable, even though the authenticity is guaranteed in writing. Beginning collectors, who might not know whether an autograph is the real thing or not, would be wise to avoid such purchases.

Author signings are a great a way of collecting authentic autographs. Hundreds of Colin Powell's admirers waited hours in line at a McLean, Virginia bookstore to buy a signed copy of his autobiography. Michael Landon's daughter Cheryl autographed her book (*I Promised My Dad*) for others and me after speaking at the church I attend.

As my son Andy moved up through the ranks of Little League baseball, we would plan the family vacation to coincide with the annual induction of major-league players and others into the National Baseball Hall of Fame and Museum in. Cooperstown. According to a historical marker in the upstate New York community, Cooperstown is "where baseball was invented and first played in 1839."

Most of the living Hall of Fame members attend the induction ceremonies and, with so many celebrities gathered in one place, chances of getting their autographs are pretty good.

Andy and I would stake out the Hotel Otesaga, where the players stay, or await their arrival at the Hall of Fame museum, to try to get their signatures. Between us, we got autographs of pitching ace Bob Feller, speedster James (Cool Papa) Bell, broadcaster Mel Allen, baseball commissioner A.B. (Happy) Chandler, and many others.

We made these treks to Cooperstown seven or eight years in a row. Over the years, some Hall of Famers seemed reluctant to give their autographs—something they used to do freely. Like other sports celebrities, they have discovered that their signatures constitute a cash cow and they're milking it for all they can get.

For me, the highlight of our annual visits to Cooperstown occurred in 1982, the year that home run king Henry Aaron was inducted into the Hall. Doubleday Field was temporarily closed to visitors, but Andy and I found an unlocked door to the stadium and went in unnoticed. We had the field—a regulation-size, major-league playing field—to ourselves.

Andy went to the pitcher's mound and threw me his best stuff—a sizzling fastball, a breaking curve, and a floating knuckler that sank just before home plate.

Andy was 13, going on 14. And for a brief moment, I was the same age.

26

Moving On

But I have gotten ahead of myself. Rewind to my days with the *Telegram and Gazette*. While I was happy with the opportunity to sharpen my feature-writing skills, I found the newspaper's salary abysmally low and opportunities for advancement precious few.

Meanwhile, I learned the *Gardner News* was looking for a staff reporter. I applied for the job and was hired at $65 a week. The *News* salary was not much more than I had earned at the *Telegram & Gazette*—it was a $5 raise—but I felt the change would serve me well. The beats were the same—city hall, the mayor's office, police station, local politics, and sports.

At the *News,* I initiated a column called *Meet the People,* a regular weekly feature focusing on ordinary folks from all walks of life. I fit in well with the Gardner scene, and I had a talented editor in Alvah Abbott.

But for whatever reason I felt restless and dissatisfied, a common characteristic of adult children of alcoholics. I had always believed that "a man's reach should exceed his grasp," as Robert Browning said, and I was willing to take chances.

When I abruptly left the *News* six months after joining it, I'm sure that some people—particularly my parents—were dismayed and wondered if I would ever amount to anything. Yet, that's when I got the biggest break in my journalism career.

Without so much as a hint that it might be looking for a reporter, I drove to Boston and appeared unannounced at the offices of United

Press International. Stanton Berens was the Boston bureau manager; Henry (Hank) Minott was the New England news manager.

As it turned out, Minott was a Gardner native who grew up just down the street from where I grew up and who began his newspaper career as a reporter for the *Gardner News*. Although there were no jobs available in Boston, Minott told me he would inquire of other bureaus in UPI's far-flung network. A week later, he called to say that the Dallas bureau—headquarters for UPI's southwest division—had an opening for a reporter and that the job was mine if I wanted it. The next day, I was on my way to Dallas, where I joined the wire service as a $90-a-week reporter.

The risk had paid off. UPI offered many opportunities, one of which was the potential to reach a huge readership—every reporter's dream. In my time with the wire service, I saw my stories printed and broadcast all over the world.

Some people believe that there is more to a coincidence than may appear on the surface. I am inclined to agree with that belief.

When I went to Boston and met with Minott at UPI's office, I had no idea that his career and mine were so similar. Growing up just down the street from me was one coincidence; reporting for the *Gardner News* was another. But it was not until I read his obituary in 1971 that I learned of other coincidences.

Like myself, Minott had once been a reporter for the *Telegram & Gazette*. He also had reported for the *Boston Post,* as I had, and worked in Springfield, where I was later to serve as UPI bureau manager for western Massachusetts.

Coincidence, providence, synchronicity or just plain luck. Take your pick. I'm just thankful that Hank Minott was there when I came knocking.

27

UPI

I wish that I had sought out more autographs than I did. If I had, I would have a most impressive collection. Like most journalists, I met my share of prominent people—kings and queens, presidents and prime ministers, saints and sinners.

Even so, I am happy with the portfolio of autographs that I have; they contain many pleasant and poignant memories.

When I look at the autograph of Martin Luther King, Jr., that I obtained in Dallas, I am reminded of the patient and earnest appeal he made to his followers to eschew violence to secure their civil rights. There is a better way, he told them, and he went on to explain the Gandhian concept of "nonviolent direct action" that he advocated.

"Nonviolent direct action never seeks to humiliate the opponent, only to win him," King said. "It has a way of disarming the opponent. It gives one the opportunity to secure moral ends through moral means.

"It makes it possible for one to struggle against an unjust system and yet not stoop to the level of hate.

"Nonviolent direct action is the most potent force available to an oppressed people in their struggle for freedom and dignity," he said. UPI's Dallas bureau included a number of talented newsmen, who took it upon themselves to teach me the tricks of wire-service reporting. Preston McGraw, a great feature writer, confided his secret to interviewing was to imagine he was talking to a neighbor over the backyard fence.

I'll always remember the advice Jud Dixon, UPI southwest division radio editor, gave me when I asked him how long should a broadcast feature be. "It's like a woman's skirt," he said. "Long enough to cover the subject yet short enough to be interesting."

Division News Director Jack Fallon was especially helpful to me. Fallon came to Dallas in 1961 after a number of years handling foreign news at UPI's New York headquarters. Fallon knew how to bring out the best in people, often with a word or two of praise at just the right time.

A dynamic, driving individual, Fallon had joined UPI's radio department in 1947 in New York. In 1963, it was Fallon who took Merriman Smith's call from the presidential motorcade in Dallas with word that President Kennedy had been shot.

A year after the Kennedy assassination, Fallon told a group of West Texas student and professional journalists that the news media must share responsibility with the Dallas police for the slaying of Lee Harvey Oswald.

Speaking at Texas Tech University in Lubbock, Fallon said the police "erred grievously in the handling of Lee Harvey Oswald's transfer from the city to county jail."

"But the press, radio and television itself are partly to blame for the Oswald case," he said. "The crowds of reporters and cameramen at city hall maintained a steady, sometimes almost hysterical, pressure on the police for information," making it easier for Jack Ruby to gun down Oswald.

Dallas was a transitional assignment for me. Fallon came up to me one day and said, "How do you like trout fishing?" It was his way of saying he wanted me to fill a staff reporter's position in Cheyenne, Wyoming, one of the southwest division's 18 bureaus.

I was single, foot-loose and fancy-free, and I loved UPI, so why not? I was game. The next day I was off to Cheyenne and the wild and woolly West.

While I never got around to trout fishing, I saw a lot of Wyoming in the year or so I was there. The Cowboy State was new to me, and the more I saw of it the more I liked it.

After a leisurely three-day drive north to Cheyenne through the Texas panhandle and Colorado, I arrived in the Wyoming capital, a city of about 42,000 people. Dan Doherty, who managed UPI's three-man bureau there, was glad to see me but wondered why it took me so long getting there.

"How'd you come—by way of San Francisco?" he said. No. I was just enjoying the scenery.

A couple of weeks later, while I was on duty in the office alone, I got to handle a breaking news story that made the front pages of newspapers around the country. A call came in saying that a passenger who had never flown an aircraft before was being "talked in" to a landing at the Cheyenne municipal airport after the pilot suffered a fatal heart attack.

I called the airport tower and over the phone took down the dramatic story of how the former Marine grabbed the controls of the single-engine Cessna 180, and safely landed it with the dead pilot and two other passengers aboard. I filed the story with UPI's Denver office, which broke in with it on the "A" wire—UPI's main trunk line—to send it to newspapers and broadcasters across the United States.

It was one of the top human-interest stories of the year—the kind of story that people in the news business dream about—and because UPI broke the story ahead of the Associated Press, more news outlets used our account than AP's.

There were other good stories in Wyoming, but none as dramatic as the safe plane landing by the pilot who had never flown before. The king and queen of Afghanistan flew in for a brief visit at the University of Wyoming in Laramie; the university had been assisting the South Asian country in an agricultural project. There was a shoot-out between Cheyenne police and a young accountant, who had been working on his income tax when he ran amok and started firing at people. I had an opportunity to schmooze with Massachusetts Senator Ted Kennedy about national politics. Kennedy and his wife Joan were in Wyoming for a football game between Colorado State and the University of Wyoming; a number of Bay Staters played for Wyoming and he wanted to cheer them on.

I had done well enough in Cheyenne that Fallon offered me a promotion as a one-man bureau manager in Lubbock, Texas. He didn't say it, but Lubbock was a hard post for UPI to fill. I accepted, and a few days later I headed back to Texas.

West Texas was a mother lode of off-beat, feature material—especially for a New Englander who knew little about life in the West but was curious to know more. Rattlesnake roundups, rodeos, cowboys and Indians, and one of the strangest auctions ever held—the auctioning off of a complete zoo, animals and all—were grist for the writing mill.

Stories about gunslinging desperadoes, cowboy reunions, ghost towns, and other lore of the West were in great demand in the big population centers of the East. (Indeed, many people back East believe that train robberies and OK-Corral kind of shootouts still take place, which is why movies and stories about the Old West are so popular even today.)

From my downtown office in the *Lubbock Avalanche-Journal* building, I'd first write a feature for newspapers, then turn around and rewrite it for UPI's radio and television subscribers. The difference in writing for print and writing for broadcast is in style: broadcast writing employs short, punchy sentences and is more conversational in tone.

Both sides—print and broadcast outlets—gave my features good play; at one time I led the Southwest Division in broadcast-feature output. I was enjoying the independence I had as a one-man bureau manager, and even getting used to Lubbock.

The UPI Dallas desk gave me freedom to decide what I would cover and write about in the huge territory assigned me. The area extended from Amarillo in the north to Wichita Falls in the east to Abilene in the south and El Paso in the west.

Occasionally, Fallon would spot me elsewhere when he was short-handed. During the 1964 presidential campaign, for instance, I covered a speech in Houston by Barry Goldwater's running mate (William Miller; anyone remember him?) A few weeks later, I returned to Cheyenne to cover the outcome of Wyoming Senator Gale McGee's reelection bid. But mostly, I could pick and choose my assignments.

One assignment I gave myself was an attempt to interview Billie Sol Estes, a notorious Texas financier who had found himself enmeshed in the toils of the law for alleged swindling.

Wheeler-dealer Estes was a longtime friend of Lyndon Baines Johnson. Estes had been convicted of defrauding Texans by selling them mortgages on nonexistent tanks for storing anhydrous ammonia fertilizer.

(The U.S. Supreme Court subsequently reversed the swindling conviction on the grounds that Estes's Texas state court trial had been televised over his objections, thereby violating his civil rights.)

Estes lived in Abilene. I learned his street address and called on him unannounced. He came to the door when I knocked, we talked briefly on the doorstep, but he would answer only a few questions. It wasn't the kind of interview I had hoped for but there was enough to file a story to Dallas.

I had one more post with UPI before I left the news agency; that was in Springfield, Massachusetts—again as a one-man bureau manager. Except for Dallas, none of the UPI bureaus I worked in was considered a choice assignment by most Unipressers; Lubbock, Cheyenne, and Springfield weren't exactly garden spots of America.

But they were excellent proving grounds, especially the one-man bureaus, where you could get valuable experience in your craft.

28

Storyteller Thornton Burgess

In Springfield I was in home territory. Gardner was an hour's drive away; the University of Massachusetts at Amherst, where I did my undergraduate study, was even closer. When I wasn't covering breaking news, I looked for feature material just as I had in Lubbock, Cheyenne, and elsewhere.

I hadn't been in Springfield long before I learned that bedtime storyteller Thornton Burgess was in a nursing home in nearby Hamden, a sleepy village near the Connecticut line, where he was recuperating from a stroke. Burgess brought me back to my preschool days in Brattleboro when my mother read me his stories.

The famed author of children's stories—fanciful tales about Peter Rabbit, Jimmy Skunk, Danny Meadowmouse, and other animal inhabitants of The Green Forest—was only weeks away from his 91st birthday but still as young as ever to boys and girls around the world who had heard or read his stories.

The Peter Rabbit tales have been translated into Chinese, Swedish, French, Spanish, and German and are still sold in bookstores today.

From time to time, the Burgess stories were cliffhangers, but they were never violent; they always had a happy ending, which made children see the world as a safe, warm place.

When I was a very young boy, my mother read Burgess's stories to me at bedtime in hopes that I would drift off to sleep without much fuss. It worked; I was captivated by the tales, and usually nodded off before she had finished.

I felt that a feature story pegged to Burgess's birthday was a natural, and would appeal to a wide readership.

I arranged an interview, drove to Hamden and met with the nonagenarian for more than an hour. The stroke had left him in a wheelchair, and he was helpless in many ways.

"I can't write. I have no use of my left hand," he said. "I have to have someone dress me; I have to be put to bed just like a child." But he was still nimble of mind and as whimsical as any of the animal characters at Smiling Pond or Laughing Brook.

In what turned out to be one of the last interviews he ever gave—he died six months later—Burgess spoke on a number of topics, including his writing, longevity, and his definition of success.

—On his writing: "My writing is spontaneous. Usually, when I start a story, I haven't any idea at all how it's going to end. I know it's all wrong, of course. A teacher of writing would tell you that you should have a careful plot."

On longevity: "I just lead a normal life without spending too much time worrying about tomorrow. Keeping busy also helps. I do not approve of forced retirements. I see men who are active, then retire. In three or four years, they're gone. If they have a hobby, they're all right. There's nothing like keeping busy."

On success: "Success is very difficult to define. You can be a failure in other people's eyes, and still be a success. My definition of success is it's the feeling that your work is the very best you can do, and that it has been accepted."

He paused a few moments and added, his blue eyes twinkling: "Success is attaining a position in life where people tell you that you're a lot smarter than you know you are."

The feature was widely used, and I felt good about it. I felt even more so when Jud Dixon wired me from Dallas that he liked it and that "the Southwest Division has lost a good feature writer."

There's nothing better than praise from one's peer or mentor to boost self-esteem.

In the summer of 1965, Springfield was wracked by racial tensions. At about the same time that the Watts riot broke out in Los Angeles, African Americans in Springfield charged police with brutality and demanded their full civil rights under the law. The city was a powder keg waiting to explode.

As tense as the situation was, however, the lid stayed on and rioting never occurred. Unfortunately, some national news organizations, including UPI, AP, and the New York Times, erred in reporting otherwise.

The *Columbia Journalism Review,* in its fall 1965 issue, carried a piece by Springfield broadcaster Durham Caldwell titled *The PaperRiot* scolding the media for their allegedly erroneous accounts of what took place that summer.

Caldwell cited a report in the August 15 *New York Times* that said "rioting (in Springfield) broke out after police arrested 23 civil rights demonstrators blocking the steps of City Hall early Friday evening." Two weeks later, the *Times* publicly admitted its error, putting the blame on "a misleading news agency dispatch."

Caldwell's CJR article went on to quote an AP story that read: "Rioting is reported in Springfield, Massachusetts, with two stores set on fire after the arrest of civil rights demonstrators."

Caldwell said that he found "no mention of the word 'riot' in published UPI copy, but I do find what I consider inaccuracies and oversensational treatment." He singled out for criticism a UPI story in the *Boston Globe* that led with the statement, "Carloads of Negroes rolled through the streets and a dozen picketed police headquarters today as an uneasy peace followed the fire-bombing of two white-owned stores."

Caldwell asked me whether I had written that lead. I had not. I would not have worded a story that way unless I had actually witnessed the event, which I had not. I suspect that UPI's Boston desk may have hyped up the story.

At the end of that long, hot summer in Springfield, I felt burnt out. I left UPI. In doing so, I joined thousands of other journalists who have worked for the wire service or its predecessor organizations—United Press and International News Service—at one time or another in their careers. Some UPI graduates went on to become household names, among them Walter Cronkite, David Brinkley, Helen Thomas, Charles Corddry, Neil Sheehan, Hedrick Smith, and Howard K. Smith.

After leaving Springfield, I spent a couple of weeks in Gardner, then drove to Lake George, New York, for a few days' vacation. It was there that I met Carol, my future wife. I asked her to marry me but the timing was wrong.

Carol had other things she wanted to do before she married; after all, she was only 22, I was 35. She went to Aspen, Colorado, where she waited on tables and became a "ski bum." (We caught up with each other four years later and tied the knot.)

29

NANA and the Goldbergs

With Carol off to Colorado, I looked for a job. What else was new? I was lucky; I went to New York City and once again through coincidence, providence or synchronicity—I landed an interview with Sid Goldberg, news editor of North American Newspaper Alliance (NANA). He offered me a job and I accepted.

NANA was one of the oldest and most respected of the nation's newspaper syndicates. Its daily and weekend news reports were distributed to 150 of the world's leading newspapers. It was renowned for its "big-byline" articles, pieces signed by Winston Churchill, Richard Nixon, and others of their station in life.

Located on West 41st Street on the fourth floor of a building that also housed the *New York Herald Tribune*, NANA was a feature-writer's dream. As Goldberg's assistant, I edited, rewrote, excerpted, and proofread articles by leading columnists and writers of the day. I also wrote feature articles under my own name that received wide play throughout the world.

NANA's stable of writers and columnists included President Gerald Ford's press secretary, Jerald ter Horst; Washington reporters Sarah McClendon, Vera Glaser and Alan Emory; psychologist Joyce Brothers; Ernest Cuneo, a member of Franklin D. Roosevelt's "brain trust" in the 1930s, and Hollywood reporter Sheilah Graham, an intimate of novelist F. Scott Fitzgerald.

Sid was a quiet sort of a guy, whose main function seemed to be cultivating columnists and newsmakers for the syndicate. He was a frequent habitué of the Overseas Press Club, often haunted by New York movers and shakers.

At the time I joined NANA, in December 1995, Goldberg was single. Soon afterwards he met his future wife, Lucianne Steinberger, a Washington lobbyist, who gained notoriety 30 years later for her role in the Monica Lewinsky scandal that ultimately led to President Clinton's impeachment.

Lucianne came to the office occasionally, and we chatted about work and events of the day. She was brassy and loudmouthed, as I recall, clearly the dominant partner in her relationship with Goldberg.

To celebrate their engagement and forthcoming marriage, several of us in the office took the couple to lunch one day.

During the 1972 presidential campaign, Lucianne was a $1,000-a-week spy planted in George S. McGovern's press corps, sending reports on the Democratic nominee to the Nixon camp.

Much later, she was back in the news as the New York literary agent who allegedly urged Linda Tripp to tape Lewinsky's account of her relationship with President Clinton. Goldberg later became host of a New York radio talk show, *Lucianne Live*. She has since kept a low profile.

I enjoyed New York's fast pace; it was life in the fast lane. For most of my time in Manhattan, I stayed at the Dixie Hotel (since renovated and renamed the Hotel Carter) on West 43rd Street, directly across from the *New York Times* building—the "old Gray Lady" as it was called.

As many others have discovered, I found that the city could be a lonely place, especially on weekends if you were single. The excitement of the job more than compensated for this drawback, however, and some great opportunities came my way. My press pass was a ticket to movie premieres, play openings, and other events; I went on press junkets to Texas, Montreal, Puerto Rico and elsewhere, and met many celebrities.

All too often, however, I turned to alcohol to dispel the loneliness I felt. As a result, I did some foolish things that were to hurt me and my career.

As I look back on my NANA experience, the greatest professional opportunity the job offered me was the freedom to develop my own style of writing, a style I describe as spare and lean. I was continuing the process of mastering my craft. NANA subscribers were using my features with increasing regularity, a clear sign of acceptance.

I particularly liked to interview and write about people in the entertainment business, and I was in a good position to do so. Publicity agents for Hollywood and Broadway actors and producers barraged the New York news syndicates with requests for features about their clients; I could pick and choose from those that interested me.

At Sardi's restaurant, the "in" place for the stars of stage, screen and television at that time, I interviewed film producers Robert Wise and William Wyler, stage producer David Merrick, and a number of actors and actresses.

I chatted with Hollywood director John Huston about film-making at the St. Regis Hotel on East 55th Street, interviewed stage and screen star Lee Remick in her dressing room backstage at the Ethel Barrymore Theatre, and spent an afternoon interviewing music man Fred Waring at his workshop at Delaware Water Gap, Pennsylvania.

30

Flatman and Ribbon

Though opportunities abounded to obtain their autographs, I rarely thought to ask for them of the many celebrities I interviewed. Adam (Batman) West was an exception.

Like millions of other Americans, I became caught up in the phenomenal success of the Batman TV series that West starred in during the Sixties. When the chance to meet the Caped Crusader presented itself, I gave in to the child within and asked him for his autograph.

The opportunity came when West and his sidekick, Burt (Robin) Ward, came to New York to promote their first full-length Batman movie. I accompanied the Dynamic Duo on the final day of their grueling, three-day personal appearance tour of 34 theaters in the New York metropolitan area.

As the bus drove us from theater to theater, beginning in Jersey City and moving on to Greenwich Village, lower Manhattan, Harlem, and the Bronx, West talked about the perils and pitfalls of the tour and his acting career. He even sneaked in a couple of Batman jokes:

"Where does Batman go first thing in the morning? The Batroom, of course." (Duh!) "What did they call Batman and Robin after they were run over by a steamroller? Flatman and Ribbon."

At one theater in the Bronx, West's advance team felt that police protection was inadequate, and they canceled his appearance. A minor riot broke out when the crowd that had assembled learned of the cancellation.

"I've learned something about mob psychology," West said. "There's always some bad ones laying for you, heckling you and trying to see how tough you are. I've found that if you go right up to them and look them in the eye, they dissolve into the crowd."

A virtual unknown before taking the Batman role, West was disdainful of critics who called him an "overnight success."

"I spent eight years in Hollywood before Batman came along, and another seven years in radio, TV, and stage. So it actually took me 15 years to become that 'overnight success'," he said.

At the end of the day, a relaxed West pulled out a studio publicity photo of himself from his briefcase and wrote on it: "To Jim Shevis. What a ride we had! Adam."

31

Washington, D.C.

I t is not unusual for journalists to change employers now and then. As in any career field, a change is sometimes necessary to achieve a higher salary, a more prestigious beat, or a better job. Also, the desire to see new places—or just plain restlessness—keeps many journalists on the move.

Clearly, I was a mover; I had a healthy curiosity about the world around me and I wanted to know more about it. So, as may be obvious by now, I moved around a lot. Indeed, it would not be unfair to say that I've had a checkered career. (Occasionally, I can almost hear my mother's admonition, "a rolling stone gathers no moss.") At the same time, with each move I reached a higher plateau in my career field—in terms of both prestige and remuneration—and I don't regret the moves. There were more ups than downs.

At any rate, after a couple of years with NANA, I moved again, this time to the nation's capital where I accepted a copy editor's job with Newhouse National News Service.

Newspaper and magazine publisher Samuel I. Newhouse who ultimately acquired a chain of 31 dailies in 22 cities, including the Newark Star Ledger and the Portland Oregonian, between 1922 and the 1970s, owned the news service. It still has offices in Washington today.

As an editor, I supervised the copy flow of a 12-member staff that included nationally known political writers Jules Witcover and Erwin Knoll. I wrote fewer articles than I did when I was with UPI or NANA, but Washington was the news Mecca of the world and a nice place to live as well.

Located at 1750 Pennsylvania Avenue just a block from the White House, the newspaper chain had offices on the same floor as syndicated columnists Art Buchwald and Evans and Novak. Buchwald, whose office was two doors down the hall from Newhouse's, would occasionally dash into my office and ask me to copyread his column.

Once in a while, I was able to get out of the office to cover a news event. I covered a hearing at the Capitol chaired by Senator Robert F. Kennedy, and a news conference by folksinger Joan Baez at the Hay-Adams Hotel across from Lafayette Park. But mostly I was deskbound, editing and proofreading a daily report of national and international news that was distributed by wire to the Newhouse newspapers. I wanted to be where the action was, reporting the news.

32

Martin Luther King, Jr.

Unhappy with the desk job at Newhouse, I got lucky again: I landed a plum job with Reuter, the London-based wire service, covering the U.S. Senate. The job entailed going to the well of the Senate each morning the chamber was in session for a briefing by Majority Leader Mike Mansfield (Democrat-Montana) on the day's agenda, covering the most important committee and floor hearings that day, and helping out on breaking-news stories.

One of the great breaking-news stories during my time with Reuter occurred on April 4, 1968, following the assassination of Martin Luther King, Jr. Washington erupted in violence that day, and was placed under martial law as African Americans vented their anger and frustration over King's death.

A sudden eeriness swept over downtown Washington when word of the civil rights leader's death spread throughout the city that afternoon. The skies darkened and people scurried to safety.

I was stunned by the announcement of King's death. Just four days earlier, I had covered his address at Washington's National Cathedral. Now the country's most prominent advocate of nonviolent resistance to racial oppression was gone, silenced by a gunman's bullet.

I returned to my office at the National Press Building, and was assigned to street-coverage of the burning and looting that followed in the wake of King's death. I persuaded a Washington, D.C., police car patrol to let me ride with them as they tried to restore peace. It was a long, tiring evening; fear was palpable as National Guardsmen roamed the streets.

Long after midnight, Reuter reporter Dan Gottlieb and I went to
14th and U Streets in northwest Washington to report on events there.
The heart of the city's black ghetto, 14th and U was the scene of some
of the worst rioting.

The violence was understandable. King had given African Americans hope of a better day, daring them to dream that "one day this
nation will rise up and live out the true meaning of its creed—'we hold
these truths to be self-evident, that all men are created equal'." King
was gone now and, in the minds of many blacks, his dream of racial
equality and justice would again be deferred as it had been for 400
years.

Gottlieb and I stayed in the riot-torn 14th-and-U Streets corridor
until 3 o'clock the next morning. When I got home, an armored personnel carrier was parked in front of my apartment building in Scott
circle, six blocks from the White House. Drained from the excitement,
I flopped on the bed and slept until noon.

The Reuter job did not work out; we parted by mutual agreement
and without ceremony. In adjusting to life in the capital, I had made
mistakes. I was learning that, though life in Washington seemed to
move at a slower pace than in New York, it could be a tougher
city—especially if you drank as I did.

I took my failure hard, and spent the summer trying to put my life
in perspective. One day I came across a newspaper article my mother
had sent me a dozen years earlier at another dark hour in my life; once
again it helped me stop beating up on myself.

Written by a clergyman, the article led to a spiritual awakening
within me, a complete change of lifestyle and, in time, one of the nicest
autographs I've ever collected—Carol's signature on a marriage license.

"Nothing succeeds like failure," the article read. "Some of the
world's greatest victories have been born of defeat. The men who never
fail will likely never but half succeed. As the poet Keats once put it:
'Failure is the highway of success'."

Hollywood actress Rosalind Russell put it this way: "Flops are a part of life's menu, and I've never been a girl to miss out on any of the courses."

33

We Meet Again

I never expected to hear from Carol again after our parting four years earlier, but shortly after leaving Reuter I received a letter from her. She had addressed it to me in Gardner, and my father had forwarded it to me in Washington. Then living in Aspen, Carol wrote that she had read a NANA article of mine in the *Denver Post,* and suggested we renew our relationship. We corresponded, she came East and we resumed our courtship. This time, the timing was right. I proposed to her and she accepted.

Before the marriage took place, however, a miracle occurred. Still drinking and feeling down because of losing the job with Reuter, I met a young woman, a German tourist, at a hotel singles event across from my apartment building.

It was a Saturday night, and she planned to fly back to Germany the next day. She asked if I knew of a church she could attend on Sunday. I told her of Foundry United Methodist Church just around the corner from the hotel, and she invited me to go with her. I accepted the invitation, even though it had been some time since I had been to church. The next morning we walked the two blocks from my apartment building to 16th and P Streets Northwest, where Foundry is located.

Something happened at that Sunday service that I cannot adequately describe or account for to this day. It may have had something to do with the music and the fellowship, and it almost certainly had something to do with the message of redemption that the minister, Reverend Edward Bauman, laid upon the congregation.

Bauman, a brilliant theologian and one of the best platform speakers in America, was a visionary, as are all highly effective preachers, and he had a huge following. Foundry parishioners included Senator Robert Dole and his wife Elizabeth, Congressman Lee Hamilton, and other Washington movers and shakers.

(A hundred years or so earlier, when the church was at a different location, Abraham Lincoln was among its congregants. More recently, President Clinton, his wife Hillary and their daughter Chelsea regularly attended services at Foundry.)

Whatever it was—I have always thought of it as a spiritual awakening—from that day on my life changed. The young woman left for Germany, and I never saw her again.

Shortly afterwards, I quit smoking—a two-pack-a-day habit that I had had for 21 years. Six months later, I found myself still wanting a cigarette when I had a drink, and I vowed that if that's what it took to keep from smoking I'd give up drinking, too, which I did. Thank God, I have neither smoked nor had a drop of alcohol in over 30 years.

Everything seemed to work out according to divine order. The miracle—and as far as I am concerned it was nothing less—brought in its wake positive lifestyle changes. I became a new person, a regular churchgoer whose life gradually was transformed.

A year later, Carol and I married. I became a father the moment I said, "I do." Carol had given birth to twin daughters from a previous relationship. Heidi and Holly were two years old at the time of the marriage; shortly after the wedding I legally adopted them.

Three weeks before the wedding, I was still without employment. A call from an Arlington, Virginia, employment agency fixed that, however. I was offered a job as information director of the Consumer Federation of America (CFA)—a position related to journalism, but out of the mainstream. For someone about to marry, the job was a godsend. I had no trouble saying "yes" to it.

CFA was a Washington-based organization representing scores of smaller consumer groups that had sprung up across the country to protect Americans in the market place. Most of the groups operated on a shoestring budget, and were unable to contribute much to CFA's support. The AFL-CIO—the American Federation of Labor and Congress of International Organizations—was its major benefactor, helping it to get off the ground. It has since flourished and today wields a great deal of clout in the marketplace.

As CFA's first information director, I wrote press releases, arranged news conferences, responded to press inquiries, and worked closely with consumer advocates Ralph Nader, Esther Peterson, and other leaders of the burgeoning consumer movement.

I was just beginning to settle into the job—and marriage—when my life was nearly snuffed out. It happened on a bright, sunny morning in April, seven months after Carol and I had married. CFA's president, another board member, and I were enroute to Baltimore to attend a convention when a drunk driver hit our car head on. We were lucky no one was killed.

I was the most seriously injured. At the moment of impact, I was catapulted from the back seat, my head hitting the windshield. Had I worn a seat belt I might not have suffered the broken thighbone that resulted; the fracture occurred when my right leg struck the back of the front seat.

My femur was so badly shattered doctors at the Washington Hospital Center could not insert a pin to bring the bone together, the usual procedure in such a case. Instead, I spent three months in traction to allow natural healing. During that time, I suffered a pulmonary embolism that could have been fatal.

I don't know how we survived that first year of marriage, but somehow we did. Carol was pregnant with Andy when the accident occurred. For several months after leaving the hospital, I was in a wheelchair before graduating to crutches and a cane. Carol deserves credit for managing the family during that time.

CFA and I parted company shortly after I returned to work. Friends in the labor movement found a temporary editorial job for me until I could get back on my feet. The job eventually led to a permanent position as assistant editor of the *AFL-CIO News* in Washington.

34

The AFL-CIO

The AFL-CIO job was as secure as a job could be; for the next 13 years my family and I prospered materially. The salary was just as good as that paid any Washington reporter with my level of experience, and the benefits were probably better. The work also held my interest most of the time.

From my fourth-floor window, I could look across Lafayette Park to the White House where occasionally I went to cover a labor-related news conference. I wrote not only on bread-and-butter issues—contract negotiations, strikes, joblessness, occupational safety, and other topics—but on the general economy, consumer affairs, politics, and international affairs as well.

I also covered union conventions in the United States and Canada. When Jimmy Carter spoke at the AFL-CIO's biennial convention in Washington, I arranged for Carol and the children to come and hear the future president of the United States.

I was sympathetic to the union cause. As a first-generation American, I had a view of the industrialized world in which labor unions had a role to play. My immigrant father, who went only to the eighth grade in his native Scotland, brought his family through the Great Depression partly due to his membership in the Brotherhood of Railway Signalmen. I benefited in other ways.

My father's union membership helped me get a job with the Boston and Maine Railroad five summers in a row. The earnings enabled me to get through college, the first member of the family to do so. It was only natural that I would regard the labor movement with favor.

Growing up in a union household helped me get the job with the labor federation, I'm sure. But John Barry, the *AFL-CIO News* managing editor, was swayed more by my writing skills and newsman's credentials than by my union connection.

"I'd rather have someone who can write but doesn't know much about labor than the other way around," he told me during the job interview. "It's easier to teach someone about unions than to teach them to write."

Despite the job security and benefits, I was at a turning point in my career and in my life as well. Basically, I was untrue to myself in taking the job. I had always seen myself as a professional journalist, objectively reporting the news. My goal—as it is with many journalists—was to cover the White House.

In taking the job with the *AFL-CIO News*, I had veered off my career path. I had entered the world of cause, or advocacy, journalism, as opposed to commercial journalism. Whatever I wrote for the AFL-CIO would be seen as having a certain spin to it. Labor's spin.

I believed in much of what the AFL-CIO stood for, particularly its human-rights policy and its championship of the poor and underprivileged. Many people envied me my job. It carried prestige, and it provided well for me and my family. But in my own mind I had settled for less than I had aimed for. The good pay, benefits, and job security amounted to "golden handcuffs."

As the years went by, I became more and more unhappy with myself for straying from my original career path. Increasingly, this unhappiness affected my home life. Carol and I argued more, and I spent less time with her and the children.

I began to look for Washington jobs in journalism but found it difficult to make any headway while holding down a job. Instead, I turned to graduate study—a commendable pursuit in and of itself but in my case, a way of avoiding the real problem.

Over a two-and-a-half-year period, attending evening, weekend, and summer classes, I earned a Master of Liberal Studies degree at

Georgetown University. The courses I took were in the humanities, human values, and international affairs. For my thesis, I wrote an analysis of global human rights from an American perspective.

I enjoy learning, and the Georgetown program whetted my appetite for more. After receiving my MLS degree, I "rewarded" myself by going to Cambridge University in England for a three-week summer course in modern British politics and economics.

Returning home, I decided to work for a doctorate in international studies. My already strong interest in international affairs had grown stronger as a result of writing about foreign trade unions, doing graduate study, and travel. I reasoned that a doctorate would help to further my career.

For the next five years, in the evenings after work, I took courses at American University's School of International Service in Washington. I was not to receive the doctorate, however. By Spring 1983, I had completed all the necessary courses, passed the oral qualifying examination, and advanced to Ph.D candidacy; I had chosen to write my dissertation on Soviet labor unrest, and had gone to Russia with a group of A.U. students and professors to familiarize myself with the country and the Soviet system.

But not long after I came home from Russia, Carol left the marriage. That ended my studies. Carol could not take the children; she had no place to stay and no job at the time, so they stayed with me.

I was devastated. It was all I could do to manage job and home and deal with the emotional trauma of the breakup. Something had to give. I jettisoned the study program, and two years later I resigned from the AFL-CIO.

It would be years before I recovered from the marriage breakup—in large part because of the codependency baggage that I had been dragging around with me all my life.

In retrospect, I probably would have been better off if I had stayed true to my-self. As mythologist Joseph Campbell put it:

"If you follow your bliss, you put yourself on a kind of track that has been there all the while, waiting for you, and the life that you ought to be living is the one you are living. Wherever you are—if you are following your bliss, you are enjoying that refreshment, that life within you, all the time."

A few centuries earlier, Shakespeare had urged a similar tack: "Unto thine own self be true...."

Carol and I had had marital problems. Sometimes they got out of hand. We had had counseling, and somehow kept the marriage going while raising the children. The marriage had its ups as well as downs, however. We both loved the children. We made several trips together, including trips to California, Scotland, Canada and to the Adirondacks. I think she felt trapped. I am sorry that I was not there for her when she needed me; I wish I had been nicer to her.

35

My Wife, the Wryter

After she left, Carol successfully pursued a career in community journalism, notably with the *Herndon (Virginia) Times*, where she became the newspaper's senior reporter. She had also written articles for the *Herndon Observer* and the *Washington Times*. She had a natural, breezy writing style, and won several awards for her writing.

Carol had a marvelous sense of humor, and a wry way of expressing herself (her car license plate read "Wryter.") For example, on our 10th wedding anniversary, she wrote the following verses:

> *"A now epic poem, marking the occasion*
> *Of our 10 years of connubial living:*
> "We wanted to get married,
> "So a decade to the day ago
> "We said the vows and pledged our trowth.
> "*Now* we can see what God hath wroth!
> "God has a sense of humor, so
> "He wound us up, then let us go.
> "He gave us what it takes to last,
> "To look ahead, learn from the past.
> "Though life is hard and full of struggle,
> "We have each other still to huggle."

When she died February 23, 1994, I was with her in her lonely room at Georgetown University Hospital. At least I was with her then in the final moments of her life.

She was only 50 but she had seen Heidi and Holly marry and Andy on the right track following some problems he had in the wake of the divorce. She had done well in her career. And she left behind a ton of friends.

Carol will long be remembered for her contributions to the Reston-Herndon community. Janet Rems, managing editor of the *Times Community Newspapers*, said that though she had never met her, "Carol is a legend" in the Times news rooms.

A Herndon civic group dedicated a bench "in memory of Carol Shevis, writer and poet." Another planted a yellowwood tree "in memory of Carol Shevis, writer who put down roots and shared Herndon's small town spirit."

I miss her to this day. I no longer obsess over what happened between us. I contributed to the breakup as much as she, probably more so. We had reconciled three or four years before her death, and had become friends. I just think of her and the good times we spent together.

I have Carol to thank for many things—the comfort and support she gave me during the automobile accident that nearly took my life; the children, the help and encouragement she gave me in my work and studies, and for much more—not the least of which was the12-step program that she recommended to me and which helped in my recovery.

Until I started going to meetings of Emotions Anonymous (EA), I did not think I had a problem or that I in any way contributed to our marital distress. It was all her fault, I said. EA—a 12-step spinofff from Alcoholics Anonymous—taught me differently.

I had bottled up my feelings most of my life—especially anger and fear—and these emotions had a way sometimes of surfacing inappropriately. Also, I had a need to control my environment—including people, particularly those closest to me like Carol.

The main lesson I have learned over the years that I attended the 12-step meetings was that I cannot change another person. I can only change myself. For me that means realizing that I don't have to be as hard on myself as I used to be. I now try to "wear life as a loose garment."

I'm learning, also, to love myself more—a key to recovery. Something I heard Maya Angelou, the American author and poet, tell an audience at George Mason University seems to sum up the tenets of the 12-step programs:

"You've got to love yourself before you can love anyone else," she said. "The more I can love myself, the more I can love you."

At a memorial service a few months after Carol's death, Herndon Times editor Marcia McAllister asked my permission to publish a written tribute to Carol that I had planned to read to those who had assembled there. Here it is:

"Carol and I met for the first time 29 years ago. She was 22 years old and, I've just got to say it: she was a knockout.

"The place was Lake George, New York, in late September. Carol was working temporarily as a bartender below the deck of a cruise ship that plied that beautiful body of water.

"I was between jobs, having just left United Press International as its bureau manager for western Massachusetts.

"Carol was something else, even back then.

"We went out for dinner that night, and afterward drove to the lake where Carol decided she was going to go for a swim. And she did—she jumped in, clothes and all.

"Here I am, wondering what's coming off here. But that's just the way Carol was as I came to know her over the years: spontaneous and full of life—truly a free spirit.

"I left the next day, and when I got home I found her riding boots in my car. I returned the next weekend to give them to her, and wound up asking her to marry me.

"She turned me down, which was a smart thing to do. Neither of us was ready for marriage. We barely knew each other. Besides, she wanted to go to Aspen, Colorado, and become a 'ski bum,' which she did.

"I heard no more of her for four years. Then I got a letter from her. She had met someone, given birth to twin girls. She had broken up with the girls' father, and was teaching high-school English in Craig, Colorado.

"She had seen my byline on an article in the *Denver Post*. We corresponded and that summer got together again. Three months later, we were married.

"Carol brought joy into my life, and three days before she died I was able to tell her that. I asked her to forgive me for my wrongs against her, and she said, 'Me, too'.

"We were married 14 years. Like every married couple, we had our differences. Ours were too much.

"I remember once, during marriage counseling, being asked what it was that Carol brought to my life, and my answer was 'light'.

"Carol had a delightful smile and a whimsical sense of humor that—even in the darkest of times—helped to lift my spirits. She brought an added dimension to my life.

"I was with Carol when she died at Georgetown University Hospital; I was the only one there when she took her last breath. She had been battling ovarian cancer for two years and lost.

"I'd like to say she died peacefully but she was clearly in pain, even with the heavy dosage of morphine they gave her.

"I held her hand and rubbed her cheek. I spoke to her of the good times and I tried to engage her in song—mostly church songs we both liked.

"Carol loved to sing and play the guitar. But as she lay there with a tube in her nose, she could make only a brave attempt at it.

"When I sang the old camp song, *I've Got the Joy, Joy, Joy, Joy Down in My Heart,* she uttered the word 'joy' and managed to hum a bit of the melody. But she could do no more.

"The doctor came into the room, and gave her another injection of morphine. Minutes later, Carol died.

"Carol's death was untimely. She would have been 51 next month. She won't get to see her first grandchild, due in July.

"But she did a lot in the time allotted her. She gave birth to three children, who are fine young adults today. She had a successful newspaper career. She had friends. She spread her joy and her light.

"Just before she died, I whispered to her, 'Carol, do you remember—either shortly before or just after we got married—I asked you what your goals in life were and you said, 'I want to be a nifty old broad.' Well you reached your goal, kid."

That she did.

36

Big Labor's Clout

Working for the AFL-CIO was an education in itself. The 13 years that I spent with the organization were not wasted years. I learned much, particularly about how Washington works.

The federation and its crusty leader, George Meany, wielded a great deal of power—in politics, the workplace, and in communities across the United States. In the early Seventies, when I joined the AFL-CIO, *U.S. News and World Report* magazine rated Meany the nation's most powerful person after President Nixon.

Labor's backing in elections, whether national, state or local, often meant the difference between victory and defeat for an office-seeker. Candidates for the U.S. Congress and for the American presidency particularly sought the AFL-CIO's support.

Georgia Governor Jimmy Carter, campaigning for the Democratic presidential nomination in 1976, courted labor's vote all that spring and summer. He needed Meany's backing to win the nomination, and he sought it assiduously.

On May 14, 1976, word spread throughout AFL-CIO headquarters that "Carter's in the building," meeting with Meany in his eighth-floor office overlooking Lafayette Park and the White House. Afterwards, Carter fielded questions from the media in the lobby; a photographer's closeup of Carter included me in the background. (I later sent the photo to Carter's office for his autograph.)

Carter went on to win the Democratic nomination by a wide margin at his party's convention in New York, becoming the first southerner to do so since Zachary Taylor in 1848. In the November presidential election, Carter defeated his Republican opponent, incumbent President Gerald Ford.

As influential as the AFL-CIO was in the 1970s, many of its member unions were conservative and reactionary, its leaders aging and slow to get behind such issues as the rights of women, blacks, Asians, and Hispanics. To many observers, both in and out of the AFL-CIO, it seemed that organized labor had become rigid and hierarchical—as hidebound as any government bureaucracy.

Labor's failure to seek new members in the fast-growing service sector of the economy, until it was too late, cost it heavily. Membership dropped off and it lost much of its former clout with employers, Congress, and the White House.

George Meany was a private person. If you met him on the elevator at the AFL-CIO's 16th Street headquarters in northwest Washington and said "hello," his usual response was an unintelligible grunt; it wasn't that he was anti-social, it was just his nature.

He had a good sense of humor, and a George Burns-like sense of timing. Once, at a union convention in Washington, the 85-year-old Meany began his remarks by saying:

"Thank you, thank you. I'm glad to be here this morning. (Pause) But then at my age I'm glad to be anywhere." An unoriginal joke, perhaps, but Meany's timing and manner of delivery brought down the house.

Meany died the following year, 1980, and was succeeded by AFL-CIO Secretary-Treasurer Lane Kirkland.

Because of its failure to adjust to the changing economy, the AFL-CIO saw its membership drop to 13 million in the mid-Nineties, its lowest level since 1969 and little more than the 12.6-million members it had at its founding in 1955.

Where the AFL-CIO scored some of its most stunning successes was not at home, but overseas. Both Meany and Kirkland lent their considerable muscle to helping free-trade unions abroad that were struggling to survive under authoritarian or totalitarian regimes.

The AFL-CIO's steady support of Solidarnosc (Solidarity)—the Polish independent trade-union federation led by Lech Walesa—was a classic example of the help given foreign labor unions by the federation. It was a running story, one that I wrote about from the very beginning of Solidarity's rise in 1981.

Solidarity's ascendancy to power was the first crack in the Iron Curtain, and was instrumental in the ultimate demise of communism and the breakup of the Soviet Union. The AFL-CIO deserves much credit for its backing of the Polish labor union.

The federation's support of Solidarity was consistent with U.S. labor's longstanding policy on human rights. From its founding, the American labor movement has stood for justice, freedom, equality, and human dignity.

In a labor magazine published four months before he died, Meany noted that "the first rights to be taken away by dictatorships of both the right and the left are those which are the lifeblood of both free trade unions and democracy: freedom of speech, freedom of association and assembly."

From time to time, the AFL-CIO invited leading Soviet dissidents to address its members, among them Aleksandr Solzhenitsyn, Vladimir Bukovsky, and Andrei Amalrik. I usually was assigned to cover their visits. (While I did not get Solzhenitsyn's nor Bukovsky's autograph, I twice obtained Amalrik's; years later, I also got those of two other high-profile Soviet dissidents, Andrei Sakharov and Yuri Orlov.)

At a 1975 Washington dinner organized by the AFL-CIO to honor Solzhenitsyn, the exiled Russian novelist praised the American labor movement for opposing the Ford administration's policy of detente toward the USSR. The Nobel laureate urged U.S. unions to hold to their strong anti-communist position.

Ironically, the AFL-CIO's overseas involvement led in part to Kirkland's ouster in 1995. John Sweeney, who successfully challenged Kirkland for the federation's presidency, was part of a faction within the AFL-CIO that felt the federation should limit its activities abroad and spend more of its time and resources at home, especially in organizing new members.

37

Bumps in the Road

I left the AFL-CIO in 1985. Leaving the federation was not an impulsive action; I had given it much thought over the years. Carol and I had divorced the year before and, like others who have gone through a similar trauma, I felt the need for change.

As I looked back over my years with the organization, I had done well. In 1982, the Washington-Baltimore Newspaper Guild awarded me first prize for articles I had written about the AFL-CIO's protests over the communist crackdown on Solidarnosc;

Who's Who in Labor included me in its 1976 edition, and I had made friends throughout the Washington establishment.

"To every thing there is a season, and a time to every purpose under the heaven (*Ecclesiastes* 1-1)," I said at an office farewell lunch in my honor. It was time once again to move on, even though I did not know where I was going.

C.B., a friend of mine in Emotions Anonymous, used to say, "We're never more safe than when we don't know where we're going." What he meant was that, when we seem to have lost our way, that's when God is there looking out for us—even though we can't look out for ourselves. I fastened on to that, and it has helped me through the years.

I had not lined up another job, thereby breaking the first cardinal rule in a jobseeker's creed; I just wanted to get away from a place where I had felt so unhappy. I wanted a fresh start somewhere else. I had an idea that I could earn a living as a freelance writer from my suburban Washington home; to a certain extent, I was successful at that.

Through my labor contacts, I got work writing and editing a newsletter for the American Institute for Free Labor Development, the foreign-affairs arm of the AFL-CIO organized to train young trade-union leaders from Latin American and Caribbean countries; I also picked up other work, including a feature-writing assignment for *Airline Pilot*, a monthly magazine of the Air Line Pilots Association (ALPA), an AFL-CIO union.

What I had not counted on was the loneliness that confronts many freelancers, nor had I fully dealt with the emotional trauma of the marriage breakup. Three months after I left the AFL-CIO, when an opening as managing editor of *Airline Pilot* magazine developed, I applied and was hired for the position.

The road soon became bumpy again. Six months after I was hired, ALPA "reconfigured" the magazine staff and eliminated the managing editor's job—an early version of the "downsizing" that was to mark the U.S. economy in the 1990s. I was out of work once more.

Once again my luck held. A few weeks after leaving ALPA, I found a part-time job with the Fairfax County (Virginia) government as co-editor of its biweekly employee newspaper, *The Courier*. It was just what I needed at that time—an anchor that would allow me time to freelance.

Over the next two years, I wrote articles that appeared in the *Christian Science Monitor*, *Washington Post*, *The Journal Newspapers*, and other publications. I also wrote regularly for the *Courier*, which won five national awards for news and feature articles during my tenure with the newspaper.

Neither the freelance writing nor the part-time job paid much, given the Washington area's high living costs; I had trouble making the monthly mortgage payment. But together they enabled me to hew to the writer's creed: *"nulla dies sine linea"*, Latin for "never a day without a line," or, freely translated, "a writer should write every day" to succeed.

At the same time, I combined the part-time county job and freelancing with an adjunct professorship at George Mason University in Fairfax, Virginia, teaching advanced composition to juniors and seniors. It is true, as I had heard over the years, that teachers often learn more from their students than students learn from their teachers. Teaching writing to others honed my writing skills and prepared me for the next leg of my newsman's odyssey.

38

USIA

O rren Peterman, deputy chief of the Near East and South Asia branch of USIA's Wireless File, looked at my resume and said: "Why do you want to give up what you've got now? It looks like you have a pretty good deal."

I had answered a *Washington Post* classified ad for a writer-editor in the Near East branch of the United States Information Agency's Wireless File. Now here I was, in the spring of 1988, being interviewed for the position.

The question, coming from the man who would be my supervisor if I were hired for the job, really made me think: what *would* I be giving up? The *Courier* job had flexible, part-time hours and relatively little pressure; it also provided an opportunity to teach and to freelance. But I yearned for something more.

I'd long been guided by Chief Justice Oliver Wendell Holmes, Jr.'s dictum: "As life is action and passion, it is required of a man that he should share the passion and action of his time at peril of being judged not to have lived." For me, that translated into a career in journalism, a field that had allowed me to share in "the passion and action" of my time.

It didn't take me long to reply to Peterman's question, however. The Middle East was where the action was, and I wanted to better understand the tangled events that were taking place there. He seemed pleased with the answer, and a few days later he called and offered me the job. Peterman later told me that my UPI experience had swayed him in my favor.

Little known to the general public, the Wireless File—since renamed the Washington File—has been called USIA's "newspaper to the world"; it is one of the tools the agency used to enhance worldwide understanding of the American people and their government.

USIA no longer exists. It was abolished and folded into the State Department in October 1999. It has a new name—the Educational and Cultural Bureau—but its function remains the same: "telling America's story to the world."

The File distributes news articles and editorials appearing in the U.S. press, articles produced by USIA writers and editors, and important official texts and transcripts from the White House, State Department, and the Pentagon to some 250 U.S. embassies and consulates around the world. Selected items are made available to foreign media and government officials.

The report is produced Monday through Friday in Spanish, French, Arabic, and Russian as well as in English, and transmitted via electronic means.

The File is older than the agency itself, older too than the better known Voice of America, a separate USIA division. Established by the State Department in 1935, the File was made part of USIA when the agency was created in 1953.

During World War Two, USIA was known as the Office of War Information (OWI). Much of OWI's efforts were unabashedly propagandistic; after all, the United States was in a struggle to the death with the Axis powers and, as the saying goes, "all's fair in love and war."

The agency has suffered unfairly, I believe, as a result of its OWI lineage. Its critics charge even today that it is a propaganda tool of the U.S. government. I would dispute such a charge. I was never told to manipulate nor distort the truth, and I know of no one else who was either.

The agency rightly takes credit for its role in the collapse of the Soviet Union and the downfall of communism, but to my knowledge it never resorted to lies or half-truths to attain that end; VOA broadcasts often were the only source of legitimate news that people behind the Iron Curtain had about the outside world and their own countries.

While both the File and VOA—the latter now part of the International Broadcasting Bureau—still operate today, federal budget constraints have forced a cutback in their activities. Also, with the end of the Cold War, serious soul-searching in Congress, the White House, and USIA itself over the agency's mission led to questions about USIA's viability in the "new world order."

As government offices go, USIA was relatively free of the inhibiting regulations and red tape that I had experienced in the Air Force 40 years earlier. Which is not to say that it was without its frustrating, bureaucratic procedures. Getting promoted, resolving a grievance or getting reimbursed for out-of-pocket expenses could take weeks, months or years.

Once I learned the system, however, my level of frustration subsided and I was able to enjoy my job. Working for the File was much like working for UPI or Reuter: there were deadlines to meet, a writing style to follow, and news sources to develop.

What I especially liked about the File was the professionalism, competence and camaraderie of the two dozen or so writer-editors who made up its staff. These were men and women who had worked for AP, UPI, Reuter, the *New York Times*, the *Washington Post* and other top-flight news organizations. As government journalists, we were a bit out of mainstream journalism, but in an honorable calling nonetheless.

One of the staff writers was Paul Malamud, the son of Pulitzer Prize-winning novelist Bernard Malamud (*The Natural*). Paul was a great writer in his own right, even in his father's shadow.

My first week at USIA provided an opportunity to obtain the autograph of Jeane J. Kirkpatrick, U.S. permanent representative to the United Nations during the Reagan administration.

I had told Peterman how much I enjoyed "street" reporting—i.e., getting out of the office and covering an event—and the next day he assigned me to cover a downtown panel discussion in which Kirk-patrick was a participant.

Before the discussion got under way and while the panelists were adjusting their microphones, I asked the former Georgetown University political-science professor for her signature, which she gave me.

Sponsored by the American Enterprise Institute, a conservative Washington think tank where Kirkpatrick was a senior fellow, the discussion turned on whether there had been a shift in U.S. public support for Israel in the wake of the nine-month-old Palestinian uprising, or "intifada," against Israeli rule and, if so, would it affect the direction of the Middle East peace process.

Talk of the peace process had seemed interminable for so long that I wondered whether peace would ever come to the Middle East. Just when hope for a settlement appeared on the horizon something seemed to happen to prevent it from coming about.

As I listened to Kirkpatrick and the other panelists debate the issue, my mind drifted back a generation to a lovely fall day in Williamstown, Massachusetts, where another U.S. diplomat pondered the difficulty of achieving peace in that region of the world.

John Foster Dulles, secretary of state under President Eisenhower, spoke of the dangers to peace posed by Egypt's takeover of the Suez Canal at an October 6, 1956 Williams College convocation. I had read that the college was to award him an honorary degree, and had dropped by to hear his speech.

I arrived at the entrance to Chapin Hall where the ceremony was to be held at the same moment as Dulles; I gave in to an impulse and asked him for his autograph, which he gave me on a sheet of notepad paper.

Dulles's remarks on world peace are as valid today as they were then. He warned the nations of the world to live together in harmony or suffer the consequences.

"War will be an ever-present danger until there are better developed institutions for peace," he said. "Waging peace is as difficult a task as waging war. Mankind will never win lasting peace so long as men use their full resources only in tasks of war."

39

Street Reporter

In my year-and-a-half with the Near East and South Asia branch of the File, I reported and wrote on a wide variety of subjects and events. I got my wish: I did a lot of street reporting, covering the arrival and itineraries of government leaders from India, Israel, Egypt, Pakistan, and other countries in the region.

Among the visitors were Israel's Yizhtak Rabin, defense minister at the time, later the country's prime minister, who was assassinated in 1996; Prime Minister Yizhtak Shamir; Abba Eban, former Israeli ambassador to the United States; Ariel Sharon, Israel's newly elected prime minister, then the country's Minister of Trade and Industry; Egyptian President Hosni Mubarak; Egyptian Foreign Affairs Minister Boutros-Boutros Ghali, who was later to become U.N. secretary-general, and Pakistani Prime Minister Benazir Bhutto.

Like most journalists, I have long felt that I could cover and write about any subject. I believed that my preparation as a journalist and subsequent experience in the craft equipped me to do that with authority and style. USIA gave me the opportunity to demonstrate that ability.

Besides staking out a foreign leader's arrival on the National Mall, reporting his or her sidewalk remarks at Blair House or a speech at the National Press Club, I wrote background articles and feature stories that involved lengthy interviews and research.

The feature I most enjoyed writing was a 4,200-word article in remembrance of India's Jawaharlal Nehru on the100th anniversary of the Indian prime minister's birth. The article had been requested by the American embassy in New Delhi for publication in *Span*, its four-color monthly magazine.

Before starting to write, I interviewed more than a dozen American writers, academicians, journalists, ambassadors, and other "old India hands" whose lives had touched the Indian statesman at one time or another. I wanted to write a word portrait of the great leader drawn from their reminiscences.

Among those with whom I spoke were John Kenneth Galbraith, U.S. ambassador to India from 1961–63; writer Norman Cousins, who served as an aide to Nehru at the 1955 Bandung conference on Afro-Asian unity in Indonesia, and the wife and children of Chester Bowles, another American ambassador to India.

In the process of collecting anecdotes about the Indian leader, I felt that I had come to know him as a person. We shared many of the same likes and values.

Samuel Bowles, the ambassador's son, recounted an especially poignant vignette. He recalled from his father's memoirs that when Nehru died there was found on a table near his bed these lines, in Nehru's own hand, from Robert Frost's poem, *Stopping by Woods on a Snowy Evening*:

> "The woods are lovely, dark and deep,
> "But I have promises to keep,
> "And miles to go before I sleep,
> "And miles to go before I sleep."

Bowles, an economics professor at the University of Massachusetts in Amherst, added:

"When you think that what Nehru held dearest to him at the time of his death was a fragment of verse by a very American poet, when there was a wealth of Indian poetry from which he might have chosen, it suggests the internationalism of his heart. He was truly a global person.

"When the day comes that an American president will have a poem in Sanskrit lying on his bedside table, we will have made great progress toward peace and international understanding."

The Nehru article was well received. *Span* led its November 1988 issue with the piece, accompanied by photographs. At their request, I mailed copies of the magazine to Galbraith and Cousins, who sent back flattering comments about the article.

"My congratulations on an article of uncommon value," Cousins wrote. "The essential Nehru comes through in your piece—the intellectual grandeur of the man; the natural aristocracy combined with a genuine understanding of the needs and passions of people; the sense of history and the sense of fun. The writing is of a very high order. I was pleased to be included in the piece."

Galbraith: "That is a very nice, indeed touching, piece. Thanks ever so much for sending it—and for our pleasant encounter."

The former ambassador to India asked that I send a copy of the article to Hollywood actress Angie Dickinson, whom he had mentioned in the piece. Dickinson later sent me a note of thanks.

A personal note:

During my conversation with Cousins, I took the liberty of telling him how devastated I was by my divorce and that I had not yet recovered from the hurt. Cousins had written a best-selling book, *Anatomy of an Illness*, on how he had overcome a life-threatening disease by maintaining a positive attitude.

"You'll heal," he assured me. "You will. Just emphasize the use of humor and all the other positive emotions such as love, faith, and trust," he said.

His words seemed to help and by practicing his advice, I slowly but surely began to heal.

40

Stormin' Norman

J ournalists meet many interesting and "important" people in their work, and reporters for the Wireless File were no exception. During my years with USIA, I met or interviewed scores of ambassadors, members of Congress, high-level State Department officials, international leaders of government, and celebrities in a variety of fields.

Journalists are not the only ones who get to meet such individuals, of course; they just have more opportunities. The average Washingtonian runs into the rich and powerful too. Indeed, they do so with such frequency that they tend to become blasé about it; they see them in restaurants, supermarkets, and on the streets. In good weather, it was not unusual to see President Clinton, surrounded by Secret Service agents, jogging near the Tidal Basin.

But even the most blasé Washingtonian would stop and stare at the late John F. Kennedy, Jr., or Madonna. For me, the stopper was Desert Storm hero H. Norman Schwarzkopf.

"Stormin' Norman," as he was called by his troops, was one of the most interesting people I met during my years as a USIA reporter. We met in October 1988, two years before Operation Desert Storm got under way in the Persian Gulf.

When he first sat down next to me in the Foreign Service Institute classroom in Rosslyn, Virginia, I had no idea who he was; nor did any of the other government officials there for an intensive study course on the Near East. He was quiet but affable and dressed in civilian clothes.

Later in the morning, when Schwarzkopf had stepped out of the classroom, FSI instructor Peter Bechtold whispered to us that Schwarzkopf did not want to attract attention by wearing his Army uniform. He wished to be treated like any other member of the class, Bechtold said.

Outwardly, that's the way faculty and students treated him for the rest of the course; once his identity was known, however, the deference shown his rank and position was palpable.

Schwarzkopf had enrolled in the course to update his already considerable knowledge of the Middle East before heading up the U.S. Central Command. He was to become commander-in-chief of all U.S. forces in the Middle East, with headquarters at MacDill Air Force Base, Tampa, Florida. CENTCOM's headquarters were located in Florida because the Gulf nations did not want U.S. bases on their soil.

I had signed up for the course to learn more about the region I wrote about for USIA. I drew the seat next to Schwarzkopf because of an alphabetical seating arrangement.

If I had not been told otherwise, I would not have taken him for a three-star Army general. (He received a fourth star after assuming his new command at MacDill.) He seemed like just a "regular guy" with whom I felt at ease; there is not necessarily any inconsistency there: one can hold high rank or office and still be a "regular guy."

I did not hold him in awe, but I was impressed with this man who would later lead American military forces into battle against Iraq's Saddam Hussein. In a personal reflection after the Gulf war broke out, I wrote the following article for the File:

"'A four-star general sits next to me. He's to be commander-in-chief of all U.S. forces in the Middle East. He is Norman Schwarzkopf.

"I wrote this note to myself two years ago, on October 17, 1988, on the first day of a Foreign Service Institute (FSI) area-studies course on the Near East in Rosslyn, Virginia. Why? I hadn't met that many four-star generals, to be truthful, and I was impressed by the awesome responsibility he was to take on within two months.

"On reflection, though, I was also impressed by the unassuming nature of the man who now heads up our American military forces in the Persian Gulf. He was 'a regular guy', someone with whom you felt at ease.

"Stormin' Norman,' as he's called by the troops, never flaunted his rank during the two-week course we took together. Not once did he appear in class in uniform, for instance; he wore casual civilian clothes.

"At the time, Schwarzkopf was deputy chief of staff of the U.S. Army for operations and planning, in charge of anything and everything that had to do with the Army worldwide.

"During coffee breaks, or when we went for lunch at the Rosslyn Eatery, we talked about a number of things—baseball, for one; it was around World Series time, and we both enjoy the game.

"We also talked about the Near East and the tinderbox it had become. He knew what he was getting into.

"Sometimes our chats took a philosophical turn. Once we talked about the spiritual side of man, which he said he believes in. Another time we talked about the curves life throws at us—and the definition of success, something people often differ about.

"'There are two kinds of success,' Schwarzkopf said. 'There's the success people see you as, and the success you see yourself as being'."

"The second kind was the one that mattered more to the general."

I sent the general a copy of the story, which he liked. "Thanks for your complimentary reflections!" he wrote back in his own hand. "I'll try to live up to them."

The Schwarzkopf persona that I saw did not square with that described by some others, and I need to point out that I saw him under different circumstances than they did. The man I saw was in a controlled environment; he was friendly, gentlemanly, self-assured, and humble.

A friend of mine, who was at MacDill while Schwarzkopf was there, said that she saw him as a pompous and self-seeking individual; she expressed surprise when I told her my impressions.

Colin Powell, chairman of the U.S. Joint Chiefs of Staff and Secretary of State under George W. Bush's administration, dealt with

Schwarzkopf almost daily during Desert Storm. In his book, *My American Journey* (Random House), Powell wrote that "Norman Schwarzkopf, under pressure, was an active volcano." That's what produced the nickname, "Stormin' Norman," Powell said.

"I recognized the root of his rages," Powell said. "Blowing up acted as a safety valve for his frustrations. For all his pyrotechnics and histrionics, however, Norm was a brilliant officer, a born leader, and a skilled diplomat in the region."

41

A Trip to Paradise

Until the early Nineties, when Congress began wielding its ax on the federal budget, USIA journalists routinely traveled abroad to report on major news events. While the budget cuts dried up much of the agency's travel funds, File reporters still traveled a good deal.

White House reporter Al Sullivan usually was aboard Air Force One whenever the president of the United States left the country; State Department reporter Russ Dybvik traveled with the Secretary of State, and a File branch reporter almost always accompanied the U.S. vice president when he toured a region.

I itched to travel but did not get the chance until I switched to the File's East Asia and Pacific branch. Even then, another year-and-a-half was to go by before I actually went on an overseas trip; it was one worth waiting for, however.

The Federated States of Micronesia is a chain of islands in the Western Pacific about halfway between Hawaii and the Philippines, lying seven degrees north of the equator.

Of the country's 607 islands, only 65 are inhabited; these 65, in turn, comprise the nation's four states (island groups) of Chuuk, Pohnpei, Kosrae, and Yap. FSM's capital is at Palikir on Pohnpei, the largest of the islands.

Largely undiscovered by tourists because of its remote location, Micronesia is everyone's idea of a tropical paradise. It is lush and green, with year-round temperatures in the 70s and 80s. There are breathtaking views of waterfalls, white, sandy beaches, and swaying palm trees, all of which contribute to a serene and relaxed way of life.

Tourists—especially Japanese, Australian, and American—are gradually finding Micronesia on the map, however, and the Micronesian government has high hopes that others will too. It is in a region of the world where ecotourism has especially great potential.

Ecotourism is partly what led me to Micronesia. I had written a story in early 1991 about Bob and Patti Arthur, the owners of a Micronesian resort hotel who had been singled out by the U.S. Overseas Private Investment Corporation (OPIC) for its first ecotourism award.

OPIC—a federal agency that promotes American investment abroad—praised the Arthurs for the manner in which they had built and operated The Village Hotel on Pohnpei.

The Arthurs had built 23 thatched "ihmws," or bungalows, in the Pohnpeian rain forest, leaving the trees standing and planting the units among them. The bungalows were situated to take full advantage of the spectacular view of the island's reefs and lagoons as well as the prevailing breezes.

"They are legends in Pacific Islands tourism because they run a sound, profitable business and exhibit a social conscience and a commitment to the environment that governs their business practices," OPIC said of the Arthurs.

The OPIC award, presented to the Arthurs at a Capitol Hill reception in June 1991, came at a time when USIA was debating whether it could afford to send a reporter to cover the South Pacific Forum.

The Forum is an annual get-together of the leaders of 15 Pacific Island nations to discuss issues of common interest. Following their meeting, larger nations with interests in the Pacific—the United States, China, Japan, Britain and other European Community countries—engage in a dialogue with the islanders on issues in which all have a stake.

The 1991 forum was to be held in Pohnpei, with the Federated States of Micronesia serving as the host nation.

The case was made by the powers-that-be in USIA's East Asia and Pacific area office, as well as in the area branch File, that the conference was of sufficient importance to U.S. interests that a USIA reporter should go to Pohnpei. I got the nod because of my earlier story on the Arthurs.

Pohnpei is a long way from Washington, D.C., nearly halfway around the world. Getting there was both exciting and educational. After an overnight stay in Honolulu, I left on a Continental Air Micronesia flight to Pohnpei. Stops along the way were at Johnston Island, Majuro and Kwajalein atolls in the Marshall Islands, and Kosrae in the Federated States of Micronesia.

An American soldier carrying an M-1 rifle met the plane at Johnston, a speck in the Pacific Ocean where U.S. chemical waste from World War Two has piled up over the years. The Pacific Islanders believed that the waste posed a threat to the waters that surrounded them.

No one was allowed to get off the plane at Johnston because of the tight security on the island but when I asked if I could just step onto the concrete runway to be able to say I had been there, the guard said "okay, but just for a second."

At Majuro and Kwajalein, dozens of Marshall Islanders poured onto the plane. At Kosrae a Peace Corps Volunteer (PCV) came aboard. PCVs first came to Micronesia in 1966 and, in smaller numbers, were there in 1991, living with host families in small communities and passing on their skills to the people.

A driver from the U.S. embassy met me at the airport in Pohnpei, and drove me to The Village Hotel, where I had an "ihmw" reservation. Along the route, several rusting World War Two Japanese tanks lay by the roadside. They had been damaged in U.S. air attacks during the war, and were deliberately left there as reminders of Japan's long occupation of the island. Japan occupied Pohnpei from 1914 until 1945 when it was liberated by American forces.

The Federated States of Micronesia is a self-governing nation under a Compact of Free Association with the United States, a unique arrangement in relations between nations. The Marshall Islands has the same arrangement with the United States.

The Pacific trip was immensely valuable to me. I learned more about a part of the world I had never seen before and could only dream about. The adventure also provided me an opportunity to become more proficient with the information technology today's reporters must master if they are to stay on top of their profession. I marveled at the way my stories were instantaneously transmitted over a telephone line from a tiny Pacific island to a computer queue in downtown Washington.

The assignment boosted my self-confidence. I felt that I had hit my stride at the agency. I had shown my USIA supervisors that they could send me out on any assignment, foreign or domestic, and I'd deliver the story.

42

Al Gore

Government journalism wasn't the commercial journalism I would have preferred; it's what's called cause or advocacy journalism. But the cause—"telling America's story to the world"—was a worthy one.

At least I was closer to my original career path than when I was with the labor movement. I had become more accepting of where I was too. What helped me arrive at that point was the support I got from my supervisor, Bill Durham.

One of USIA's most senior staffers with over 30 years with the agency, Durham believed in me more than I believed in myself at times. By giving me increasingly difficult assignments and showing his confidence in my ability to carry them out, he helped me grow on the job.

The Pacific trip was a warmup to more challenging and exciting assignments ahead. Unlike the Near East and South Asia branch, where there was really only one issue to write about—the protracted peace process—the East Asia and Pacific branch abounded in news-worthy topics.

Among these were the issues of Americans imprisoned or missing in action during World War II, the Korean war and in Vietnam; concerns over rising Japanese investment in the United States, and the long-standing debate over whether to grant permanent normal trade relations status to China.

The POW/MIA issue was a painful one for relatives of missing or imprisoned. Americans; I saw this in their faces at the lengthy Senate hearings on the subject. They felt their government had not told them the truth about U.S. soldiers and airmen unaccounted for in the war.

In the summer of 1992, at the annual meeting of the National League of Families of American Prisoners and Missing in Southeast Asia, their anger reached a boiling point and spilled over into the proceedings. Demonstrators interrupted President Bush's speech with chants of "no more lies."

Bush, who had promised the emotionally charged audience full disclosure of all relevant information about the POW/MIAs, nearly lost his composure and told the protesters to "shut up and sit down."

Besides reporting running stories, such as the POW/MIA hearings, I interviewed a number of prominent people during my two-and-a-half years with the East Asia and Pacific branch. They included Senators Al Gore and John McCain; Peace Corps Director Elaine Chao; Fang Lizhi, China's foremost scientist and dissident; African American leader Jesse Jackson; William K. Reilly, administrator of the Environmental Protection Agency; consumer advocate Esther Peterson; Jessica Tuchman Mathews, vice president of World Resources Institute, and many others.

Long before I joined USIA, I had developed a strong interest in environmental protection. Environmental issues were priority concerns of both the Consumer Federation of America and the AFL-CIO, two of my previous employers.

I had also launched a column on the environment for *The Observer*, a weekly newspaper in Herndon, Virginia. The column sparked renewed community interest in the environment. Tree-Action, a local environmental group, awarded me a certificate "for journalism of significant value, responsibly crafted with care and commitment."

At USIA, writing about the environment was part of my job description.

This interest in the environment led me to interview then-Senator Gore, the leading "green," or environmental advocate, on Capitol Hill on two separate occasions.

The first interview was in the spring of 1990 as Gore was preparing for the Interparliamentary Conference on the Global Environment in Washington, which he chaired. The second meeting occurred two years later with publication of his first book, *Earth in the Balance: Ecology and the Human Spirit,*

Gore was a delight to interview. A former journalist, he responded to my questions in a thoughtful, grammatical, and quotable way. During our meetings in his Senate office, he came across as a clear thinker with a first-rate mind, at ease discussing any subject. While the interviews focused on environmental issues, they also touched on religion, family, the economy, and the writing craft.

Gore had given a lot of thought to the environmental crisis confronting the world, a crisis he described during the book interview as "an outer manifestation of an inner crisis that is...spiritual."

"We've somehow come to the conclusion that we're separate from the earth—above it all, disconnected from the physical world, and living in the world of intellect instead," he said.

"It is this separation from each other, from other communities, and from the ecological web of life that leads to the spiritual crisis. Global warming, depletion of the ozone, destruction of the forestland, and all the other ecological crises are really just symptoms of the deeper, underlying spiritual crisis."

A journalist for seven years before coming to Congress in 1976, Gore talked about the hard work involved in writing a book and offered this advice for aspiring authors:

"Writing a book requires a lot more stamina than writing daily articles for a newspaper. If you get behind on a newspaper story, you can just stay up late and finish it.

"With a book, you've got to plan your activities for years in advance, and you've got to conceive of the finished product as having an arc that starts at the beginning, goes through the body of the book, and ends where it's supposed to.

"You've also got to conserve your energy and attention span and abilities in a book and carefully work at a responsible pace so you can get it done."

Earth in the Balance took two years of research and another year to finish, working every day into the evening and every weekend, he said.

I had brought along a copy of the book, and when he saw the large number of dogeared page markers I had in it, Gore said, "Gee, you've really read the thing!"

He signed the book, "To my friend Jim Shevis, who shares my views on the environment. Best wishes, Al Gore."

Gore gets a bad rap, I think, from critics who complain that he has a "wooden" personality. I found him quite engaging, with a good sense of humor. Even more unfair, I believe, is the criticism he gets for his Bible-centered, personal values.

In my interviews with him, he made it clear that he cares for morality and family values. In a time when American morality lies in a cesspool, I believe we ought to be thankful for someone like Gore with his emphasis on character and spiritual values.

Gore cited a passage in the *Book of Psalms* to describe what *Earth in the Balance* was about. "It's about my spiritual beliefs and my religious tradition which teach that the Earth is the Lord's and the fullness thereof," he said.

"I believe that the Earth belongs to its Creator," said Gore, a member of the Southern Baptist church, "and we who were put here have a responsibility to be good stewards.

"In the face of environmental vandalism on a global scale, it's not enough for us to say, 'we were asleep, we weren't paying attention, we were too busy paying attention to other things, like ourselves',"

As for his role as vice president, I believe he filled the office better than any other vice president in the 20th century. I, for one, believe his wealth of experience would have made him a great president and regret he lost the campaign to George W. Bush. Perhaps he will get another chance at the position in 2004.

In trying to separate himself from President Clinton's relationship with former White House intern Monica S. Lewinsky, Gore spoken publicly of his displeasure about the scandal that nearly brought the country to a standstill in 1999. That may well have hurt him politically with former President Clinton and the liberal wing of the Democratic Party.

Referring to "that awful year we went through," he told reporters on the eve of his announcement that he was a candidate for the Democratic presidential nomination, Gore said: "I felt what the president did, especially as a parent, was inexcusable."

I admire Gore's candor and courage for speaking his beliefs. He is not perfect but who is?

43

Covering the Ambassadors

In the spring of 1992, the U.S. ambassadors to five Southeast Asian countries—Malaysia, Thailand, Singapore, Indonesia, and the Philippines—embarked on an unprecedented trade tour of the United States. Their goal was to awaken American companies to trade and investment opportunities in that fast-growing part of the world.

At first, it was like pulling teeth for USIA to find the money to send a reporter along on the ambassadors' trip, but in time the funds were found. I suspect discovery that President Bush had suggested the trip on his visit to Singapore two months earlier may have had something to do with it.

I was tapped for the assignment, which turned out to be one of the high points of my USIA career.

Accompanied by their chief commercial officers, the envoys crisscrossed America, holding all-day seminars in Portland, Oregon; Chicago; Detroit; Atlanta; Houston; New York City, and Washington, D.C. The two-week trip was funded by major American companies, and cost taxpayers nothing except salaries.

It wasn't that the United States was doing no business at all in the region; it was just that America was not keeping up with competition in the region from Japan, Korea, and Taiwan.

As Paul Cleveland, former U.S. ambassador to Malaysia, told the droves of businessmen and women who attended the all-day seminars: "We're back here because you're not out there. The big boys know about the opportunities and are already out there."

155

The other envoys and their posts were Frank Wisner, the Philippines; Robert Orr, Singapore; David Lambertson, Thailand, and John Monjo, Indonesia. They made a good team; each had a style of his own. Cleveland's straightforwardness, Monjo's breadth of knowledge, Wisner's suaveness, Orr's flamboyance, and Lambertson's penetrating mind were all part of the mix.

By the end of the tour, which I covered from start to finish, the ambassadors had met with executives of more than 2,000 companies as well as the governors of Oregon, Illinois, and Georgia; state commerce department officials; mayors; community leaders, and trade association officials.

The cross-country swing—the first-ever domestic trade mission—produced record-breaking press placement in Southeast Asia. Stories I wrote about the trade tour resulted in 79 newspaper placements—an all-time high for the Wireless File.

USIA video news coverage of the tour was shown on national television in several Southeast Asian countries, and the Voice of America aired reports on its English and Asian language broadcasts.

In a joint letter to President Bush at the end of the trip, the ambassadors praised USIA's role in the highly successful trade tour.

"We received record-setting coverage as a result of USIA's outstanding distribution of daily reports on our progress," the envoys said.

"We believe this had highly positive foreign-policy benefits among Southeast Asian leaders and businessmen, who warmly welcomed our growing trade and investment in the region."

Kudos for my reports on the ambassadors' tour poured in from many quarters, including the USIA leadership. The assignment proved to be a springboard to promotion.

The step-up to senior writer-editor meant leaving the East Asia and Pacific branch, where I had enjoyed a rich variety of assignments. But my new job in the European branch was just as challenging.

Much of the European branch's focus in the summer of 1992 was on fast-breaking developments following the collapse of communism and the breakup of the former Soviet Union; the vicious war in the former Yugoslavia was beginning to vie for equal attention.

Just as I was settling into the job, an opportunity arose to go to Geneva, Switzerland as an official member of the U. S. delegation to the 49th session of the United Nations Human Rights Commission conference. I was the delegation's speechwriter during the commission's five-week meeting, assigned temporarily to the Department of State.

While I had little speechwriting experience, I felt confident I could handle the assignment. I was picked for the position largely because of my human-rights studies at Georgetown and my reporting background.

I was three days late for the February 1, 1993 opening session, and not in the best of health upon arriving in Geneva. I had come down with bronchitis—"possible pneumonia," my doctor said—and for a time I considered not going at all. The opportunity was too good to pass up, however, and with some prompting from family and friends, I was on my way.

I'm glad I went. Had I not gone, I would have missed out on some rich experiences. It took me a week to recover from the bronchial condition, jet lag, and lack of sleep, but eventually I began to feel better and ready to get down to work.

Ferraro also arrived late and was recovering from a bout with the flu. The first woman nominated by a major party to be vice president of the United States. She and I quickly became acquainted.

Our offices were next to each other on the fourth floor of the U.S. mission, with a door between us that we kept open most of the time. It became clear to me shortly after my arrival that my main speechwriting duties would be to help her. Ambassador Richard Schifter, the head of the U.S. delegation, preferred to write his own speeches. Schifter's deputy, J. Kenneth Blackwell, and China expert Merle Goldman occasionally needed my assistance, but mostly I helped the former congresswoman from the Queens, New York.

(Blackwell, a former Cincinnati mayor, made history in 1999 when Steve Forbes, a candidate for the Republican presidential nomination in the year 2000, named Blackwell national chairman of his campaign, thus making him the first African American to head the presidential effort of a major white candidate.)

GERALDINE FERRARO, THE FIRST WOMAN NOMINATED BY A MAJOR POLITICAL PARTY (DEMOCRATIC) TO BE VICE PRESIDENT OF THE UNITED STATES, WAS A PUBLIC MEMBER OF THE DELEGATION. THE FOLLOWING YEAR SHE WAS NAMED U.S. U.S. AMBASSADOR TO THE UN BODY.

I enjoyed working with Ferraro and I think she felt the same about me. Upon our return to the United States, she sent me an autographed photo of herself, with the inscription, "To Jim Shevis: Thanks for making me sound so smart."

Generally, I would draft the speech, and she would add any personal touches she cared to make. That was never the end of it, however. A copy of the draft would then go for review to the State Department in Washington, where a half-dozen or more bureaucrats would look it over; invariably, they would make some alteration.

The first speech I wrote for Ferraro was on the abuse of minorities the world over. The speech went through seven revisions before State gave its final approval; about 80 percent of the original draft survived, which was better than par for the course.

"Everyone seems to feel a need to okay what's written, a need perhaps to justify their position. It's the 'system,' so I'm not going to take it too seriously," I noted in my journal.

Ferraro was a plain-spoken woman, who generally did not hide her feelings. In a draft speech on the Convention on the Rights of the Child, which the United States had not signed, she expressed optimism that the new Clinton administration would soon acquiesce in it.

When State cabled that it was "inappropriate for Gerry to express her personal 'optimism' that the U.S. will sign/ratify the Convention," Ferraro exploded: "B......! That's my opinion. I'll say what I want."

Ferraro made her mark in Geneva, championing the rights of women as well as children, condemning "ethnic cleansing" in the Balkans, and defending human rights everywhere. The following year she went back to Geneva as head of the U.S. delegation with the rank of ambassador.

I decided I had had enough red tape to last me a while, and for that reason I did not seek the Geneva assignment when it came up the following year.

Ferraro subsequently ran unsuccessfully for public office from New York, and was a panelist on the TV show *Crossfire*. She later joined a Washington-based public affairs and lobbying firm.

44

Travels with Al

Journalists tend to travel a lot. I've been in 44 of the 50 American states and 30 countries of the world. Others have traveled more, some less.

In 1993, when the White House announced that Vice President Gore and his wife Tipper would be visiting Russia, Kazakhstan, and Kyrgyzstan—countries that I had been writing about from Washington for some time—I persuaded USIA to let me go on the trip.

The purpose of the trip, which was scheduled for December 11–18, 1993, was to pave the way for President Clinton's European trip the following month.

Kazakhstan and Kyrgyzstan were places of mystery to me, countries I had yearned to visit ever since I first heard Borodin's haunting symphonic poem, "On the Steppes of Central Asia." I was also curious to see how Russia had changed since my 1982–1983 visit there with a group of American University students and professors.

The Gore trip was important for U.S. relations with Russia and the two Central Asian nations. The vice president was to attend a Moscow meeting of the Joint U.S.-Russian Commission on Cooperation in Energy and Space, which he chaired jointly with Russian Prime Minister Viktor Chernomyrdin.

In Almaty, Gore signed an agreement with Kazakhstani President Nursultan Nazarbayev providing American assistance for Kazakhstan's denuclearization. The vice president's visit to Kyrgyzstan was to show America's strong support for that country's transition to democracy.

Getting an okay to cover the trip and actually going on it were two different matters. White House politics and inexperienced staffers nearly blocked me from making the tour.

Coming as it did in the first year of the Clinton administration, the Gore trip was laid down by "kids" at the White House who were largely untrained in handling logistics of this sort. True, they had the experience of campaigning for Clinton and Gore in the 1992 presidential election but the vice president's European tour was not a political campaign. It was public diplomacy.

Many of these young people got their White House passes as a reward for their work in support of the Clinton-Gore ticket. The election was over, but their main goal still seemed to be to garner as much favorable domestic publicity for the White House as they could.

As a result, I was unable to get a seat on the vice president's plane. Air Force Two would accommodate only representatives of the commercial press—among them, William Safire and Rick Berke of the *New York Times*, Jeffrey Smith of the *Washington Post*, David Burnett and Claudia Dowling of *Life* magazine, Larry McQuillin of Reuter and John King of the Associated Press, later senior White House correspondent for CNN.

The bottom line, never stated in so many words, was that USIA File coverage would not yield a lick of publicity for the vice president back home in the United States. That was because of a congressional mandate forbidding distribution of USIA articles and broadcasts within the United States. (The government's policy has since changed, and USIA transcripts, texts and other materials are now available to the public on the Internet.)

Consequently, the White House allotted Air Force Two's preciously few seats to those news organizations that would bear the vice president the most fruit. For a while, it looked as if USIA would be out in the cold.

We did it anyway. I convinced USIA's higher ranks to let me map out a commercial flight path paralleling Gore's itinerary and report on his activities along the way. For the most part, it worked.

Poor visibility due to heavy snow prevented Air Force Two from making its scheduled landing at Almaty. Instead, it flew on to Bishkek, the capital of Kyrgyzstan, 45 minutes away. I had arrived in Almaty the night before to be on hand for Gore's arrival in the Kazakhstani capital. Had I been on Gore's plane with the rest of the traveling press, I could have covered his meeting with Kyrgyzstani President Askar Akayev in Bishkek.

The rest of the vice president's trip went smoothly enough. After a brief visit in Bishkek, he came to Almaty where he and Nazarbayev signed a number of agreements—the centerpiece being the pact providing U.S. aid to Kazakhstan in dismantling its nuclear arsenal. Then he was off to Moscow and St. Petersburg.

I wrote several stories during my three-day stay in Almaty, including one based on an interview with William H. Courtney, the U.S. ambassador to Kazakhstan. Telephonic arrangements were not compatible with my laptop computer, however; instead of filing the stories directly to Washington by telephone, as I would have done under normal circumstances, I Faxed them. But that was a minor hitch.

Timing was important if I were to successfully carry out my duties. Despite travel delays, language problems, and severe winter weather conditions in Central Asia and Russia, I managed to get to where I was supposed to be at the right time. Luck, coincidence, or whatever was with me.

For example, the Kazakhstan Airlines plane that was to take me 2,000 miles west to Moscow sat on the runway at Almaty for more than two hours before snow let up enough to take off.

I knew that Gore planned to meet with Russian President Boris Yeltsin at the Kremlin that afternoon at 3 o'clock, Moscow time, and brief the traveling press on their talks afterwards. The briefing promised to be newsworthy because Gore was sure to be asked his views on the results of the Russian parliamentary elections a few days earlier. In that election, ultranationalist leader Vladimir Zhirinovsky and his Liberal Democratic Party polled far more votes than many observers had expected.

I began to feel edgy. Would I get there in time for the briefing?

Four-and-a-half hours later, the aging Aeroflot liner touched down at Domodedovo airport outside Moscow. The U.S. embassy in Almaty had asked that someone from the embassy in Moscow meet me to help with luggage and transportation to a downtown hotel. I spoke no Russian beyond a few conversational phrases, and needed the assistance.

No one showed up at the airport; I was on my own. I managed somehow to find a taxi to take me to the Radisson Hotel, where I had a reservation and where the embassy had set up a press room. I arrived in the nick of time—more precisely, about two minutes before the vice president opened his news conference.

Sure enough, Gore was asked for his views on the elections and the significance of the large vote for Zhirinovsky and his party. In no uncertain terms, Gore denounced Zhirinovsky's extremist views in a number of areas, including the use of nuclear weapons.

Zhirinovsky had blamed foreigners for Russia's economic problems. He also had urged use of nuclear weapons against Germany and Japan if they tried to intervene in Russia's internal affairs.

"Let me say clearly for myself and on behalf of our administration and our country, the views expressed by Zhirinovsky…are reprehensible and anathema to all freedom-loving people," Gore said.

Gore's remarks were the stuff of which front-page stories are made, which is what happened. My story on Gore's briefing of his meeting with Yeltsin reached USIA posts around the world before they got their morning newspapers, scooping the *Washington Post* and the *New York Times* among other newspapers.

To say that I was satisfied with my reporting of the vice president's trip would be an understatement. I was having fun, "following my bliss," as mythologist Joseph Campbell might say. The coverage earned high praise from USIA officials—including my supervisor, who summed up the trip as follows:

"If anyone reading this evaluation has ever arrived by air in far-off Almaty, capital of Kazakhstan on the Chinese border, or in the remote forest around Moscow at one of the grim, domestic 'Soviet' airports, they will have an idea of the unusual courage and flexibility of this superb professional, Jim Shevis.

"Although there was no space on the official plane when Vice President Gore visited the NIS (Newly Independent States) in December, Mr. Shevis, who initiated the idea of Wireless File coverage of this important visit, elected to make the trip using commercial flights and local transportation and made all the arrangements himself.

"While the rest of the traveling press went comfortably on Air Force Two, the unpampered Mr. Shevis got by on his own resources and turned out a series of nine major stories, one of which enabled all our European and NIS posts to learn, before they got their newspapers, about Gore's condemnation of the ultranationalistic views of Zhirinovsky, who had done surprisingly well in the parliamentary elections held on the eve of Gore's arrival in Moscow.

"I offer the above as an example of the professionalism, flexibility, and dedication of Jim Shevis, who is considered by his peers on the Wireless File as one of its best writers. The European File could not ask for a better writer with a deep background in U.S.-European political/military, NATO, and developmental affairs."

I was subsequently nominated for the USIA director's exceptional writing award for my coverage of Gore's trip.

While my stay in Russia was brief, I could see that the political and economic climate in Russia had changed dramatically since my visit there a decade earlier. In 1982–83, the Cold War was still on, the Soviet bloc intact, and communism ensconced as the nation's political philosophy.

There were chinks in the wall that Moscow had thrown up around life in the Soviet Union, however, one of which I had focused on in my doctoral studies at American University in the 1980s. Then, reports were seeping out of labor unrest, including strikes, particularly among the coal miners. The AFL-CIO, my employer at the time and a strong opponent of the Soviet system, was tuned in to listening posts that tended to confirm the country was nowhere near the "workers' paradise" that it would have the rest of the world believe.

At the time of my second visit to Russia, in 1993, the Soviet Union had come apart and the Cold War had ended. Moscow still seemed an eery place to me, but the paranoia that I sensed in the streets 10 years earlier was of a different kind. Xenophobia ran rampant then. In 1993, the average Muscovite was more concerned about deteriorating living standards. In their efforts to install democratic capitalism, Russia's rulers were having tremendous problems keeping the citizenry fed, clothed and housed. Gangsterism was on the rise, and the benefits of the new economic system rested with a few.

45

Buyout

With such high praise for my work, why did I leave USIA a year later? There were several reasons. One was a decision to accept what is called in our "downsizing" economy a "buyout"—a financial incentive to give up one's job in a move to pare the size of the government's workforce.

Thrice in 1994, the agency offered eligible employees an opportunity to retire under its so-called "voluntary separation incentive" plan. Under the plan, the government would pay them up to $25,000 each to leave. The Clinton administration was committed to cutting the size of the federal workforce to reduce the federal budget; if workers voluntarily left, there would be less need to lay off employees.

I qualified for the buyout, as well as for retirement, even though I had been with the government only a relatively short time, about seven years. But I had reservations about the offer. I enjoyed my work at USIA; I was well paid, and well regarded by my peers and supervisors. Yet, I had come to believe that I had gone as far as I could, and that doing more of the same would not help me grow professionally.

In any event, after rejecting it in May and again in August, I accepted the agency's offer, effective December 31, 1994. What made the difference was the turmoil and confusion that accompanied the restructuring of the Wireless File.

Transformed into the Information Bureau, the Wireless File was trimmed to operate with fewer people. The bureau also abandoned the traditional, top-to-bottom style of management in favor of a team-style of management aimed at giving workers "empowerment"—part of the

Clinton administration's push to "reinvent government." The result was chaos and poor morale; the buyout appeared more enticing.

Since the I Bureau came into being, it seemed to function more smoothly, although former colleagues have told me there is still a lot of confusion in how it is run with low morale in its wake. In a further cost-cutting measure, USIA was abolished and made a bureau of the Department of State in October 1999.

"The hard facts are that Congress and the Clinton administration decided that it won't spend the money on these activities that it did in the Cold War, and the president has decided that government is going to be downsized and made more efficient," USIA Director Joseph D. Duffey said in a *Washington Post* article.

Rather than put up with all the turmoil involved in reorganization, I chose to leave and, as Robert Frost noted in his poem, *The Road Not Taken*, that "has made all the difference."

46

After the Buyout

I wasn't sure what I would do when I left USIA. But, remembering C.B.'s remark at Emotions Anonymous meetings that "we're never more safe than when we don't know where we're going," I felt everything would work out well. I had gone to a retirement planning seminar before leaving the agency, and had picked up some ideas there. (A recurring theme: "Go South," where living costs are 25 percent lower than in the national capital area.)

Beyond teaching my writing course at George Mason University, however, I could not say precisely what I would do next with my life. (I am still trying to figure that out!)

At a farewell luncheon in my honor, I told colleagues: "For two or three months or so, I'm going to step back and reflect on life a little. When the spirit moves and I get tired of doing nothing, I'll do something."

Spirit was not long in moving. The teaching course occupied only a small chunk of my time and, conditioned by a New England work ethic, I began casting about for a fulltime job in journalism or one at least related to the field.

I turned down interviews for a press secretary's position with a U.S. senator and two congressmen. Their political views were either too conservative or too liberal for my liking. Besides, though I did not realize it at the time, I could not have taken a job with any of them unless I repaid the government the $25,000 buyout bonus.

Under terms of the buyout, I could not return to the government for five years unless I repaid the bonus in full. The restriction applied to all branches of the federal government—executive, legislative and judicial.

One of the lines I had cast out netted an offer from the Washington-based Free Trade Union Institute (FTUI) to go to Zagreb, the capital of Croatia, to help that country's labor unions function better in a free society.

A foreign-affairs arm of the AFL-CIO, FTUI conducted educational programs throughout Eastern and Central Europe and in many of the former Soviet republics.

Formerly a constituent republic of Yugoslavia, Croatia declared its sovereignty and independence in June 1991, ending four decades under communism. The following month, the Yugoslav republic of Serbia moved aggressively against Croatia; bitter fighting continued off and on through mid-1995, when Croatia regained territory it had lost to the Serbs four years earlier.

As in other emerging democracies, Croatia's trade unions looked to the West—particularly the United States and Germany—for counsel, education, and material assistance to get on a firm footing in their new environment.

FTUI liked my labor pedigree and offered me a job as its country director in Croatia, a position of some prestige for I would be the representative of the American labor movement. The position was to be funded by the U.S. Agency for International Development for a year.

Not certain that the job was right for me, I accepted the offer on a contingency basis. I would go to Zagreb for a week, conduct two seminars on worker rights and, after returning to the United States, decide whether to go back for a full year's assignment.

Croatia was still a dangerous place. A couple of weeks after I returned to the United States, a BBC correspondent was killed by a sniper's bullet. Rebel Serb forces controlled about one-quarter of the country, and had launched rocket attacks on Zagreb two months before my arrival. The State Department had issued an advisory warning to Americans against traveling in the country because of the possibility of further attacks.

Calm prevailed during my week in Croatia, however. The 900-year-old city of Zagreb was enjoying summer weather, and people crowded into Ban Jelacic Square to sip coffee and gossip. I delivered my seminars, first in the small community of Duga Resa, 35 miles from Zagreb, and then in the capital.

In the end, I decided against returning to Croatia, not only out of concern for my safety, but also because of a desire to stay in my career field of choice—journalism—rather than the labor movement.

Returning from Croatia, I went back to George Mason University to teach my undergraduate writing course. I also spread my net for a fulltime job in mainstream journalism.

My hopes rose when I came across a National Public Radio ad for an off-air, senior foreign editor in Washington. I felt that my USIA experience, together with my broadcast-writing experience with UPI, well qualified me for the position. As it turned out, NPR filled the job in-house. However, I did some substitute editing while regular staff members went on leave.

In my brief stay at the radio network, I struck up an acquaintance with Tom Gjelten, who had covered the war in the former Yugoslavia for NPR since 1991. Gjelten and I had a mutual acquaintance in Gordana Knezevic, a Sarajevan journalist. Gjelten knew Gordana in Sarajevo, where she was deputy editor of *Oslobodjenje*, the city's leading daily newspaper. She later moved to Zagreb, where she joined the FTUI staff, and was of great help to me while I was there.

Continuing the job search, I learned that CNN was considering hiring a reporter to cover the federal regulatory agencies in Washington. I had two interviews with CNN before they decided not to establish the beat after all.

While waiting in CNN's "green room" to be interviewed the second time, Patrick Buchanan and Jesse Jackson—both veterans of presidential primary campaigns—walked by, engaged in conversation; they were at CNN to tape their TV shows.

I asked Republican Buchanan to autograph my business card, the only thing I had handy, which he did; I had gotten Democrat Jackson's autograph three years earlier after interviewing him for USIA.

47

Retirement

Retirement is a state of mind. You need to prepare for it to really enjoy it. Most people look forward to it as did the nation's first president, George Washington. It is "as necessary to me as it will be welcome," he once said.

In retrospect, I can see that I was not psychologically ready to retire—that is, in the sense of "removing one's self from circulation," as Webster's dictionary defines the word "retirement."

I viewed my departure from the government as a tactical move to gain greater financial stability. I never intended to take retirement lying down or sitting in a rocking chair. I also saw it as an opportunity to launch a freelance writing career.

In a later chapter, I give some further thoughts on retirement. Suffice it to say for now, however, that I have never fully adjusted to retirement. It has been a challenge.

I have kept busy but not as busy as I'd like. I've taken several computer courses; done some genealogical research; taught writing at the college level; read a lot; made home improvements; achieved "competent toastmaster" status in Toastmasters International and pursued my interest in the Civil War.

I've been successful as a freelance writer. As chief writer for News-USA, a national news syndicate in Falls Church, Virginia, I've written numerous feature articles that appeared in newspapers and magazines around the country. The articles have touched on a wide spectrum of topics and personalities, including aging, travel, the "Seinfeld" television show, Frank Sinatra and Oprah Winfrey.

48

Drug Czar Barry McCaffrey

One of the most interesting writing assignments was based on an interview of Barry R. McCaffrey, the nation's so-called drug czar. Some excerpts:

"For more than three decades before his confirmation as director of the White House Office of National Drug Control Policy (ONDCP), McCaffrey served his country in the military. You might say he was born and bred to it.

"His father, William J. McCaffrey, a three-star Army general, no doubt influenced his son's choice of career—a calling that began as a 17-year-old West Point cadet. From then on, he rose meteorically through the ranks, doing his father one better by earning a fourth star for his Army uniform.

"When he retired from active duty to take on the drug czar post, the 57-year-old McCaffrey was the most highly decorated and youngest four-star general in the Army. What he learned about war and military strategy from four combat tours (two in Vietnam) fit him admirably for the position of ONDCP director.

"I was promised only a half hour with him, but McCaffrey warmed to the discussion, and—disregarding time—spoke freely and at great length on a number of topics regarding the battle against drug abuse.

"McCaffrey began the interview by saying he did not like the 'war on drugs' metaphor. 'It's inadequate to describe this terrible menace facing the American people,' he said. He prefers the notion of 'a cancer affecting American community life.'

"Shortly after his nomination as drug czar, in February 1996, he expanded his views on the matter before a Senate committee.

"'Wars are straightforward,' he said. 'You identify the enemy, select a general, assign him a mission and resources, and let him get the job done. In this struggle against drug abuse, there is no silver bullet, no quick way to reduce drug use or the damage it causes.'

But how do you account for the astronomical rise in the use of illicit drugs among Americans over the past three decades? Reliable data show that, in 1962, fewer than four-million Americans had ever experimented with illegal drugs. Today, over 80 million are said to have tried them.

McCaffrey agreed with the figures, and said:

"'We have a changing society, and a revolution in the 1970s that included, among other things, widespread exposure to marijuana, cocaine, LSD and other drugs. It took us the better part of 15 years to get this under control.

"'The reason people experiment with these drugs is they like the effect they have on the brain; it changes the brain's neurochemistry and gives them enormous, intense, artificial pleasure. The downside of it is it's addictive. It causes bizarre social, legal, and medical problems. It changes relationships, and it turns many into compulsive users. They've now rejected illegal drugs. They don't want their children using them; if they're employers, they don't want their employees involved in them. They personally have been exposed to drugs. Thirty-million Americans have used cocaine, and an even higher number—72-million—have been exposed to marijuana.'

"'There will always be a demand for drugs,' he told me. "'Some portion of every population will continue to use illegal drugs to escape reality, experience pleasure, follow peer pressure, chase a misguided sense of adventure, or rebel against authority, among other self-destructive reasons.

"'We won't achieve total victory on drugs,' he said. "'We shouldn't expect that. We can't take every heroin or crack addict and necessarily cure them of their addiction. But we darned sure should expect to reduce the number of young people using drugs by enormous amounts and to reduce the damage that this epidemic does by great amounts'."

McCaffrey said treatment as opposed to long-term incarceration for hard-core addicts holds more promise.

As the interview drew to a close, the question arose: "'Do you get discouraged when, even though drug abuse in the United States has declined dramatically, your detractors say the 'war on drugs' is lost and can never be won?"

That's what a group of prominent Americans and Latin Americans charged following a Washington conference to map hemispheric drug strategy.

For the first time in the interview, McCaffrey drew himself up full in his chair and showed a trace of anger.

"'That's an excellent way to ask the question,' he said. "'I personally feel these are unexamined assertions. They are feel-good approaches. They are ill-thought out. It's reflective of people who know the cost of lots of things but the value of nothing.

"'These people cling to the edge of public life. They're not being held accountable for their rhetoric and, factually, it just isn't the case. We are not losing a 'war on drugs.' As I said earlier, I don't think the metaphor is very helpful.

"'A lot fewer North Americans are using drugs today than they were in 1979. And I can promise you that, in 2009, there'll be a lot fewer than in 1999.'"

49

Travels with Andy

What I've enjoyed most about "retirement," though—and having the leisure time has enabled me to do it—is travel, particularly with my son Andy. Since leaving USIA, I have traveled to Costa Rica, Croatia, China, Italy, France, Scotland, Canada, Peru, and throughout much of the United States.

My son Andy and I travel well for all our differences in age, likes and dislikes. We've been all over the East Coast, from Kennebunkport, Maine to Key West, Florida and points in between. We went to Britain in 1997, and we will probably travel to other parts of the globe before he settles down to raise a family of his own.

Despite problems we had when he was a boy of 12 and 13, Andy and I get along better today than ever. We've transcended the father-son relationship, and become friends as well. Back then, each of us in his own way, we were coping with the family breakup, neither of us fully understanding the other's pain. I like to think that, because we're older now, we're a little wiser if not more mature.

Even more than our visit to Scotland in search of our ancestral roots, I enjoyed the 3,000-mile cross-country auto trip we made the following year.

Andy had decided to leave his home in northern Virginia and settle in San Diego. I felt honored that he asked me to accompany him. I'm a generation older than he with different interests and perspectives.

Andy is a bright young man, 40 years my junior, and a computer "geek," the term these days for someone who is "into" the world of information technology. Though he does not have a college degree, he commands a good salary because of his computer skills, which are in demand these days. San Diego beckoned because of its ideal climate and a job that awaited him there.

I thought it might be fun, and took him up on his invitation. We'd take 10 days over the Christmas/New Year's holidays to get out to California, and see what we could of the lower United States. I'd always wanted to make an automobile trip across the country, and the time together would help us to know each other better.

From the outset, we viewed the trip as an adventure. It was hugely successful for several reasons: good chemistry between us, respect for each other's boundaries, a willingness to go off the beaten path, planning, getting plenty of rest, and good luck with the weather.

After an overnight visit with my daughter Heidi, her husband Ed and their 10-month-old son Benjamin in Roanoke, Virginia, we headed for Memphis. We thought we would never get there—Tennessee is one of the longest states to cross—but we finally made it. We had planned to stop at Elvis Presley's Graceland home but passed it by at the last minute due to a disagreement for which I was mostly responsible; it was our only difference on the trip.

The next day, bright-eyed and bushy-tailed, we headed for Dallas where we had a two-night reservation at the Adam's Mark Hotel. Along the way, we left the interstate to visit Hope, Arkansas, President Clinton's birthplace and early childhood home.

Built in 1917, the Clinton home is now owned by a nonprofit foundation, which had the interior decorated to resemble what it looked like when Clinton lived there, and opened it to tourists...

It was bitterly cold the day of our visit. After a bowl of hot chili, we braved the cold wind for a look around town. There wasn't much to see. As we drove off, leaving Hope behind us, Andy sighed, "Boy, I'll bet Clinton was glad to leave this place."

In planning the trip, we had three places at the top of our "must-see" list: Graceland; the Sixth Floor Museum in Dallas from where Lee Harvey Oswald is said to have shot President Kennedy, and the fast-growing gambling town of Laughlin, Nevada. We skipped Graceland, as I've previously mentioned, but we did visit Laughlin and the Dallas museum.

We arrived in Dallas the afternoon of Christmas Eve. The city was quiet because of the holiday. We were content to rest and take in a movie. On Christmas Day, we drove out to Love Field to watch the planes land and take off. The next day, we went to the Sixth Floor Museum in the former Texas School Book Depository building, which tells the story of the Kennedy assassination in photos, interviews, artifacts and documentary films.

Oswald's sniper's nest is virtually as it was the day of the shootings. It is sealed off with Plexiglas, allowing visitors to view Oswald's perch without disturbing the area.

The remainder of the trip went smoothly except for a flat tire in Arizona. There was little traffic all the way to San Diego. Often, for miles on end, Andy's Honda Civic was the only vehicle on the road.

After Dallas, we went on to El Paso, Texas, then north to Alamogordo, New Mexico to visit my brother Gordon and his family. We had not seen each other in seven years. After lunch and a brief visit with them, we headed back to the interstate.

Enroute, we stopped at the White Sands National Monument near the White Sands missile-testing range and, like little kids, had fun sliding down the sand dunes. That's where, a half-century earlier, the United States exploded the world's first atomic bomb. Important space and atomic research programs are still carried out at the testing range.

Early on, we had decided that if time allowed we would visit one of the world's great natural wonders, the Grand Canyon. Neither of us had been there before, though on a flight to Las Vegas a few years earlier we had caught a glimpse of it from five miles up. It would also give us the opportunity to visit the enchanting resort town of Sedona in Arizona's red-rock country.

It was a good decision. We tarried a few hours in Sedona before leaving for the canyon. After lunch at Bright Angel Lodge near the north rim, we took a helicopter ride over the deepest part of the canyon, marveling at the natural beauty of the geological wonder.

While grateful for the Grand Canyon experience, we were eager—like the explorers Lewis and Clark—to see the Pacific Ocean. Returning to the interstate, we drove past Williams, Arizona, and into desert country. That's where we had a flat tire. For a while, the situation seemed a little dicey: we were unable to remove the flat tire from the wheel rim.

It was dark and freezing cold, with no signs of civilization in sight. For a while, we thought we might have to spend the night in the desert. Fortunately, Andy had a cell phone, which he used to call Triple-A for roadside assistance.

While we waited for Triple-A to send someone from its garage affiliate in Seligman, 15 miles away, Andy tried once more to remove the tire—and this time was successful. We put on the spare, and were on our way to Laughlin.

Laughlin is well known in Nevada but less so outside the state, which may have something to do with the fact that the town is only 30 years old. Everything in the town grew up around Don Laughlin's Riverside Hotel and Casino, a family-type gambling Mecca where we had two nights' reservation.

To attract visitors to its casino in the slow winter months, the Riverside offers some of the best room rates available anywhere. We paid $25 the first night, $39 the second, for a large comfortable room. Besides a casino, the Riverside offers top-name entertainment. The late country-music singer Tammy Wynette had a four-night engagement while we were there.

Neither of us wanted to leave Laughlin without giving the town's golf course a try. Just minutes from the Riverside, the Emerald River Golf Course offered a challenging 18 holes of play. According to the Nevada Golf Association, the course is the most difficult course in the state. After nine holes, we knew why. The course is laid out over rough, desert terrain.

San Diego was only 370 miles away, an easy day's drive for Andy. We arrived the afternoon of New Year's Eve. I stayed for a week of sightseeing and helping Andy get settled in his condominium, then flew back to Virginia. As much as I would like to have stayed longer, all good things must come to an end.

But I'm awfully glad I went along for the ride.

MY SON ANDY WINDS UP TO PITCH IN A LITTLE LEAGUE GAME. ANDY WAS AN ALL-ROUND ATHLETE BUT BASEBALL WAS HIS BEST GAME.

50

On Writing Well

"And gladly would he learn,
"And gladly teach."

—— Geoffrey Chaucer

eaching the undergraduate writing course at George Mason University—English 302, "Advanced Composition"—is something I had started doing in 1987. It has at times been frustrating but a blessing overall. For one thing, I found to be true what I have heard other teachers say time and again: the teacher learns more than the student. Teaching writing kept my writing skills from getting rusty, and even sharpened them.

So many good books on writing are available that I would not presume to recommend more than a few I have found useful over the years.

If there is one single truth that I have found more helpful than anything else in writing, it is keep it simple.

It took me a while to fully understand this, and to practice it in my own writing. Part of the reason was that in high school and college I had the notion that the bigger, the more complex, and abstruse the words and sentences the better was my writing. I had to unlearn that after I got out in the real world of writing.

I am a strong advocate of economy of language, that is, using only words that work—eliminating those that are redundant, or simply the wrong words to use. Here, I recommend Strunk & White's *Elements of Style* (MacMillan) for more suggestions on the use of words.

Abraham Lincoln's Gettysburg address, one of the great speeches of all time, is a classic example of the use of spare and simple language. Of its 272 words, the speech contains 204 one-syllable words; 50 words of two syllables, and 18 of three or more syllables. The Great Emancipator also shied away from words of Latin origin, preferring Anglo-Saxon words instead; his Gettysburg address contained 226 words of Anglo-Saxon origin, the rest were Latin derivatives.

Writing is a skill mastered only through lengthy, arduous effort. In a way, writing is an unnatural act. By that I mean, it's not something we're born with; it doesn't come to us as naturally as breathing, walking or talking. It is an acquired skill.

In a *Washington Post* column, writer Colman McCarthy advised would-be writers to spend as much time reading as writing, with the caveat that they read only writers who know Samuel Johnson's edict: "What is written without effort is in general read without pleasure."

Finally, revise your writing, knowing that it can always be improved. Novelist James A. Michener once told an interviewer that he didn't think of himself as a great writer, "but I'm a great rewriter." Again, I like Colman McCarthy's views on the subject:

"Never trust a first draft. Never be satisfied with a second. Never think that a third is your best."

Books on writing that I have found helpful, in addition to *Elements of Style*, include William Zinsser's *On Writing Well* (Harper Perennial) and Richard Rhodes's *How to Write* (Morrow).

The classes I taught at George Mason University for the most part included full-time workers in their 20s and 30s. These were serious students, who were there on a weekend or an evening to satisfy a graduation requirement. Many knew how to write fairly well but those from other countries for whom English was a second language often struggled with their writing assignments. Fortunately, Mason's English department has a writing center offering free, one-on-one tutorial assistance.

51

Coping with Retirement

As I mentioned earlier, I have never fully adjusted to retirement. I feel I made a mistake in accepting the government's buyout offer. Before leaving my job, I recognized that social isolation could possibly be a problem for me. I am somewhat of an introvert by nature and by virtue of growing up in an alcoholic home. I would miss the interaction with my fellow workers, and would need to put some kind of structure in my day. But I measured the risk, and decided that I could cope with this new phase of life.

I had heard and read enough about retirement to know that it is a major life event akin to marriage, parenthood, divorce or loss of a loved one. It could also be looked upon as an adventure and a time of personal enrichment and adventure.

I like the definition of adventure given by Swiss psychiatrist Brian Piccard who, along with Briton Brian Jones, became the first to circumnavigate the Earth in a balloon. I use it to explain my taking the buyout:

"The definition of adventure is to accept the uncertainty, accept the anxiety, accept the doubts, prepare as well as we could, and jump," Piccard said upon completing his globe-girdling flight February 27, 1999. "It is a metaphor for life."

Yet, I was aware of the dangers of retirement and the early, sudden death that visits some retirees. A friend of mine, Al Zack, the former public-relations director of the AFL-CIO in the 1970s and 1980s, retired to Florida and died just days later.

Norman Cousins warned against retirement, saying that retirement—especially forced retirement—was one of the banes of modern American society. In a foreword to Pat York's book, *Going Strong* (Arcade Publishing, New York, 1991), Cousins wrote:

"No disease in the United States—not cancer, not heart disease, not diabetes, not multiple sclerosis—is more lethal than the boredom that follows retirement.

"The body goes into a state of rapid deterioration when it loses its reason for being, when mind and muscle are not put to use, and when the individual is surrounded by the perception of society that he or she no longer serves a useful purpose."

Cousins, who died a few days after writing the above, goes to the heart of the retirement problem. People need to feel they're of some value to society, not "just taking up space," as a retiree put it to me recently.

Retirement is not all bad news, however. Indeed, some people told me they envied my position. Often, these were people who were tired of working, frustrated with their boss and/or fellow workers, and would give anything to be free of the daily grind. It seems it's always greener in the other fellow's yard.

The keys to retirement, I believe, are to take care of yourself, stay connected with people, and keep moving. Forswear that easy chair, and stay active.

In talks with friends who have retired or are thinking of retiring, I've concluded that retirement is pretty much an individual matter—something you craft yourself to fit your own needs and likes. For some, retirement is a time to pursue a hobby or an artistic interest, to travel perhaps. It may even be the time to start a new career.

A friend, whose husband recently retired from the State Department, suggested I take day trips from my suburban Washington home. Go to Waterford, a quaint, 18th-century village in Loudoun County, Virginia, or to Camden Yards in Baltimore for an Orioles baseball game.

Another assured me that, indeed, there is life after retirement. Her husband has written one novel and is working on another. Someone else chimed in: "The idea is to have fun. Retirement is like sex: if you're not having fun, you're not doing it right."

Just before I left my job, Dede Bonner, a career consultant at USIA, gave me some good advice. She told me to "build into" my after-government plans the idea that there'd be times when I'd be figuring out what to do—and probably doing nothing. How true her advice turned out to be.

There would be mornings when I would awake and ask myself, "What did you do to yourself?" On those mornings, I questioned my judgment in taking the buyout. I felt lonely, and my self-esteem was on the floor. Other mornings, when I had a class to prepare for or an article to research and write, I was more forgiving of myself.

What kept me going was the knowledge that, at the end of five years, I would be eligible to return to government employment, which I liked because I was doing things that satisfied me. The buyout agreement stipulated that I could not return earlier unless I repaid the money. I viewed the five-year restriction as a time-out.

(Returning to government employment was not as easy as I thought. I struck out in four attempts to get back with the State Department.)

Meanwhile, I kept reasonably busy teaching, writing and reading. I got out amongst people, went to church regularly, and worked out at a health club. Also, I have worked sporadically as the chief writer for NewsUSA, a national news syndicate, for which am grateful.

I've also received enormous help and support from a men's group, which has helped me with self-esteem and to rid myself of the regrets and dark clouds I let hover over me.

I can't say that life has been a bed of roses since I embarked on this new journey. I was hurt deeply, for instance, when a woman I had known for years rejected me. But, as a counselor once said to me, "lick your wounds, get up and get going again."

52

Healthy Aging

Retirement and aging are closely linked. Some people, like my friend Al Zack, drop dead shortly after retiring; others, like my father, live on another 20 or 30 years.

Both Zack and my father retired in their 60s. But while Zack died within days after leaving his job, my father lived nearly 30 years after his formal retirement. What's more, my father continued to drink during those years and exercised very little.

While it is not altogether clear why there should be such a disparity, gerontologists who study the aging process and the problems of the aged tell us that people who are still going strong into their 80s and 90s have certain common characteristics.

Besides a healthy diet and regular exercise, these characteristics include a zest for life; staying busy; a sense of humor; no immediate intention of retiring; a healthy regard for themselves and others; involvement in some cause, or causes, larger than themselves, resiliency and adaptability to change.

Healthy aging owes a lot to economic and sociological factors. It helps to be able to afford good medical care, for instance. Staying connected with family and friends is also important.

Good genes help, too. My father was nearly 94 when he died, his mother nearly 101—sure signs of innate tendencies toward long life on at least one side of my family.

Strom Thurmond, the oldest person ever elected to the U.S. Senate, had this to say about longevity: "The secrets of health are exercise, diet, and your attitude toward life."

"There is no biological reason why we can't—all of us—live to celebrate our 100th birthday," Robert D. Willix, Jr., M.D., writes in his book, *Healthy at 100* (Shot Tower Books, Boca Raton, Fla., 1995).

"The single best thing you can do to live longer, the most powerful longevity secret of all" if you want to live to be 100 or more is, "starting now, to think you can," Willix says. "Thinking (and eventually believing) that you will live a long life sets in motion a series of other thoughts and actions that, cumulatively, will help you live longer."

According to the Census Bureau, the fastest-growing population group in the United States today is the 85-plus group. The number of Americans in that group in 1995—3.6 million—was 20 times larger than in 1900. The number of centenarians was 15,000 in 1980; their number rose to 54,000 in 1990 and is now well over 100,000.

The best move I ever made to stay healthy was to stop smoking. I remember the date I finally quit, September 18, 1968. I was 39 years old. Six months later, my next best move: I took my last alcoholic drink. Had I continued either of these life-threatening habits, especially smoking, which I had done since I was 17, I probably would have had an early death.

Since then, I have enjoyed relatively good health. While I nearly died in the 1970 auto accident, some good came of it. Though my leg was badly shattered, I vowed that I would not only walk again but would go one step better: I would take up jogging.

After my release from the hospital, where I spent two-and-a-half months in traction while the leg healed, I took short walks at first, 100 yards or so. Then I would alternate walking with jogging. Eventually, I was able to run a half-mile, then a mile.

The regimen not only strengthened my leg but also cleaned my lungs of the cigarette tars and other noxious substances that had accumulated over 20 years of smoking.

I dedicated myself to running, hitting the bricks almost every day. There was one stretch of two years when I never missed a day's jog whatever the weather. The next thing I did was to compete in 5- and 10-kilometer races, moving on to biathlons and triathlons.

All of this physical activity made me a healthier and happier person. It also illustrates the power of the mind and of exercise. In the years since I did my last triathlon—a one-mile swim, followed by a 23-mile bicycle ride and a 10-kilometer run—the leg injury caught up with me and, along with a little arthritis in my knee, kept me from competing.

The bottom line, I believe, is take care of yourself, practice moderation in all you do and hold onto your dreams. Comedian George Burns, who lived to be over 100, used to say, "if I knew I was going to live this long, I'd have taken better care of myself."

Former President Jimmy Carter, in his book, *The Virtues of Aging* (Ballantine Books, New York, 1998), makes a profound observation about getting old: "You are old when regrets take the place of dreams." Carter is a healthy 77.

And from Alsatian-born businessman and poet Samuel Ullman, this gem of wisdom:

"Nobody grows old by merely living a number of years; people grow old by deserting their ideals. Years wrinkle the skin, but to give up enthusiasm wrinkles the soul. Worry, doubt, self-distrust, fear and despair—these are the long, long years that bow the head and turn the growing spirit back to dust.

"Whether 70 or 16, there is in every being's heart the love of wonder, the sweet amazement at the stars and the star-like things and thoughts, the undaunted challenge of events, the unfailing child-like appetite for what next, and the game of life.

"You are as young as your faith, as old as your doubt; as young as your self-confidence, as old as your fear; as young as your hope, as old as your despair."

I wish I had said that.

53

A Health Scare

Even if you do everything in your power to stay healthy, however, the unexpected can happen as I discovered in the Spring of 1997.

I was enjoying lunch with my friends Gerry and Estella Bell at a French restaurant one day when Estella looked at me and, "What's that on your nose?" She had noticed a freckle on the left side of my nose that she hadn't seen before.

While I had been aware of the blemish, I dismissed it. I thought it was merely something that could be scraped off, improving my appearance. During a recent physical examination, I had mentioned it to my doctor who referred me to a dermatologist "to be on the safe side."

When the dermatologist suggested a biopsy, I felt a twinge of fear. "Biopsy" is one of those words we associate with cancer. I agreed to it, however; after all, cancer is not in my family history. What was there to fear?

Five days later, on a Saturday morning as I was planning to go away over the Memorial Day weekend, the phone rang. It was the dermatologist's office. "The doctor wants you to come in after the holiday to talk about your options," his nurse said. The biopsy had found skin cancer at "an early, early" stage.

I asked if I could see the doctor that morning; I didn't want the matter hanging over my head through the weekend. I asked if I could bring Gerry along for support. The nurse understood; she agreed, and fit me in between other appointments.

At first, I couldn't think straight. Fear and anger muddied my thinking. Life is unfair, I thought. I had gone to the dermatologist for what I thought was strictly cosmetic reasons only to be told that I needed treatment for something possibly far worse.

At the doctor's office, however, reason returned. Slowly, I began to realize that the diagnosis was a timely and fortunate one. The offending freckle was "in situ"—that is, positioned in one place—and could be cured. "The prognosis is excellent," the doctor said.

The skin condition had resulted from over-exposure to the sun as a youth. When I was a teenager, I worked five summers digging ditches on the Boston and Maine Railroad to earn money for college. Often I'd work without a shirt or head cover, almost never using a sunscreen.

In those days, getting a lot of sun was seen as healthy. You looked better, you felt better—or so you thought. Little did we know about the hazards associated with the sun's rays on the body.

We know more today. Young and old alike—especially fair-skinned people like me—need to protect themselves against the sun. Dermatologists recommend a sun block with a sun-protection factor (SPF) between 20 and 30.

How lucky I was that Estella had inquired about that freckle—and grateful for Gerry's support. Three weeks after the diagnosis, I had surgery to remove the blemish and a skin graft that is barely noticeable today. The operation was a complete success.

The experience taught me the value of friends and the importance of not overreacting when life throws you a curve.

54

Words to Live By

Finally, I'd like to pass on some sayings that have helped me on the journey of life. Maybe they'll help you as well. Here are some of my favorites:

• "I am still learning", the motto of painter-poet Michelangelo.

I am a strong believer in lifelong learning. It keeps the mind from turning to mush. I have pursued learning all of my life, whether a college or university course, an adult-education course on genealogy or an Elderhostel seminar on the Civil War. My parents used to say they did not recognize me without a book in my face.

• "Success is getting up one more time than you've been knocked down."

It's hard to do, I know. I've been there. The breakup of my marriage threw me for a loop. But when I picked myself up off the floor and was back on my own two feet—even though I felt like staying down—I was on the way to recovery.

• "Order is a lovely thing; on disarray it lays its wing, teaching simplicity to sing."

I first came across this lovely quotation in the summer of 1978 at my mother-in-law's camp at Chateaugay Lake in New York's Adirondack Mountains. It's from Anna Hempstead Branch's book, *The Work in the Kitchen*. Too often, we are prisoners of things, reluctant to let go of possessions we no longer need nor use. I have learned the simplest life is the fullest life. By minimizing the clutter, life becomes simpler and much more enjoyable.

The Shaker hymn says it all:

"'Tis the gift to be simple,
"'Tis the gift to be free,
"'Tis the gift to come down
"To where we ought to be.

"And when we find ourselves
"In the place just right
"'Twill be in the valley
"Of love and delight."

• "Be prepared."

As a Boy Scout growing up in Massachusetts, I did my best to put the Scout motto into practice. Whenever I did, good things happened. If I did my homework or studied the night before an exam, the results invariably were better than had I not prepared myself. Similarly, if I prepared for a job interview I found I was more apt to get the job.

• "A man's reach should exceed his grasp, or what's a heaven for?"

Robert Browning, the English poet, has inspired countless people with this line from *Andrea del Sarto*, including me. President Kennedy may have had it in mind when he called upon the nation to go to the moon. I have found that when I strove to achieve a seemingly difficult or impossible goal I surprised myself when I did. If I failed, I usually came close to the mark. Completing a triathlon at the age of 55 is an example; I finished dead last the first time I ran one; I didn't come in first or even ahead of those in my age group but I did finish. Professionally, my goal was to cover the White House; while I never got to cover it as a beat reporter, I did cover occasional White House news conferences as a labor or government journalist. Having hopes helps or, as poet Emily Dickinson put it:

"'Hope' is the thing with feathers—
"That perches in the soul—
"And sings the tune without the words—
"And never stops—at all—"

• "East, West, hame's best."

Whenever my parents came home from a tiring weekend trip, my mother would sit herself "doon," take a deep breath and say this short four-word Scottish saying I've remembered throughout the years.

Whether returning from a business trip to Russia or Micronesia or a summer vacation with Carol and the kids, I, too, have plunked myself "doon" and said the same thing. It was just good to be home, where I could rest and relax after a hard day's journey. Rasselas, the Prince of Abyssinia, no doubt had a similar thought of gratitude when he returned from his travels.

• "Don't be afraid to fail."

American author Elbert Hubbard, a believer in rugged individualism, wrote: "The line between failure and success is so fine that we scarcely know when we pass it; so fine that we are often on the line and do not know it. How many a man has thrown up his hands at a time when a little more effort, a little more patience, would have achieved success."

• "Four things come not back: the spoken word; the sped arrow; time past; the neglected opportunity."

Omar Ibn Al-Halif's aphorism speaks of the past and calls upon us to do the best with the time allowed us on Earth. It reminds me to use caution in what I say and do, and to be prepared for opportunities.

• "And then the day came when the risk to remain tight in a bud was more painful than the risk it took to blossom."

This observation by American writer Anais Nin squarely hit home with me for it describes my development. As an adult child of an alcoholic, I grew up in fear. Rather than talk about my fear, I held things within, "tight in a bud," which caused me immeasurable pain. It was not until Carol left me that I came out of my shell and "took to blossom."

• "Knowledge is of two kinds. We know a subject ourselves, or we know where we can find information upon it."

Journalists especially know the truth of this observation by Samuel Johnson. The best possess both kinds of knowledge; all are proficient at knowing where to find information. Journalists tend to be generalists, with a jack-of-all-trades kind of knowledge. A reporter with a specialty, such as consumer affairs, politics, foreign affairs or sports often has an edge over his peers, however. I prepared for journalism by grounding myself in the English language, which I see as a specialty. Along the way I added other specialties, including labor, consumer affairs, public diplomacy and the entertainment industry.

Conclusion

I've had a lot of ups and downs in my life. No doubt you have, too; for all our differences we're more alike than not. My "ups" have included a 14-year marriage to a woman who blessed me with two lovely daughters and a fine son. Carol's untimely death, however, was among my "downs."

On a different level, my life's "ups" included my first byline in a major newspaper (*Boston Post*); returning to college (Georgetown University) at the age of 45 and earning a master's degree; quitting smoking and drinking within six months' time; completing four triathlons; playing golf at St. Andrews with my son Andy; walking Hadrian's Wall, the 73-mile stone barrier built by the Roman emperor Hadrian to keep the "barbaric" people in Britain's north (Scotland) from raiding the south, climbing and walking the Great Wall of China, and a reasonably successful career.

As I look back on my life, I seem to have had fewer "downs," than "ups" but the "downs," when they occurred, were whoppers. Besides an addiction to cigarettes for 21 years and a drinking habit for 17, I lost a number of good jobs; suffered heartbreak over failed relationships; experienced separation and divorce, and nearly lost my life in an auto accident.

Throughout the good and the bad, I have learned to turn to a Higher Power, whom I call God, for guidance and support. That's easy to do when life is going your way; but it's not as easy when you're near despair.

Earlier, I recounted how, six months after I was married, a drunk driver slammed head on into the car in which I was a passenger. The accident occurred in broad daylight on a major highway. We were on a

201

business trip. I had started my job only a few months earlier. Carol was pregnant with Andy.

My faith then was weak, and one night when a nurse came to my hospital room to give me medication for my shattered thigh, I cried out from the darkness of my soul, "Why did this have to happen to me?"

Quietly, while she went about her duties, the nurse whispered in my ear: "Because God wanted to show you He could break you and make you whole again."

May your "ups" outnumber your "downs."

APPENDIX

I*n addition to the articles contained in the text, the following are among those I like best:*

IN SEARCH OF SCOTTISH ROOTS

A quarter-century ago, with the birth of my son Andrew, I became quite curious about my Scottish ancestry—especially about the origin of our last name, a name you won't find on every street corner. As much as possible, I wanted to be able to pass on to him knowledge of his ancestral roots.

Both my parents were born and raised in Scotland's northeast "neuk," a land area that juts out into the North Sea. He was born in Fraserburgh, a fishing community, she in Peterhead, the center of today's extensive North Sea oil-well drilling. They came to the United States 75 years ago. Beyond that, I knew little about my pedigree.

Over the years, I had collected some information. For a fee, the Scots Ancestry Research Society in Edinburgh had provided a report on my father's side that went back to 1805. Most of the males were tradesmen such as coopers and sail makers while the women generally were homemakers or domestic servants.

Also, a book on Scottish surnames that I had come across in a Boston book store on Newbury Street showed two dozen variant spellings of our last name. A Scotch whisky produced in Aberdeen—Chivas Regal—bears one of the variants. The spelling seems to have varied according to the orthography in vogue at the time or the idiosyncrasies of the chronicler.

But I wanted to know more, and a year ago I began to plan a visit to Scotland for that purpose. Andrew showed interest in going along as well if we could fit the trip in to his work schedule. An avid golfer, he was also attracted by the possibility of playing the world-famous golf links at St. Andrews where the game is said to have originated 500 years ago. So it was that in late August 1997 we found ourselves flying to Britain in quest of our origins.

The trip got off to a good start. Virgin Atlantic Airways had mistakenly assigned our coach seats to others, and to make up for the error moved us to the "upper" class section where you could get a massage or a manicure and other amenities not available in coach.

Upon landing at London's Heathrow Airport, however, we were shocked to learn of Princess Diana's untimely death just six hours earlier. After checking in at our Russell Square hotel, we went directly to Buckingham Palace where mourners already were gathered to pay homage to the "people's princess."

On the theory that to overcome jet lag you need to stay awake until your normal bedtime, we walked for hours, finally sitting down to rest at an outdoor restaurant near Shakespeare's renovated Globe Theatre on the Thames River. As we sipped tea, a camera crew from Britain's Independent Television Network came up to us and asked for our thoughts on the tragedy. It was a typical man-in-the-street interview; we did our best to express our numbed feelings.

While Diana's death cast a pall all over Britain, people went about their lives as usual and so too did we. In the week that we were in Scotland, we traveled the country from top to bottom, by train and by auto, uncovering some startling information about our ancestry. We also got to know each other better.

After a four-and-a-half-hour train ride from London to Edinburgh, where we picked up a rental car, we worked our way up Scotland's picturesque east coast to St. Andrews, a university town rich in culture and tradition and home of the Royal and Ancient Golf Club, the governing body for the rules of golf in most countries. Andy did all the driving—650 miles altogether; I could not get used to driving on the lefthand side of the road, as motorists do in Britain.

We parked the car in front of St. Andrews Castle, the medieval castle of the archbishops of St. Andrews, and as if by chance spied a bed and breakfast just across the street. After a good night's rest there, we set off for the House of Schivas, a 15th-century castle near Tarves that I had heard about for years.

The House of Schivas is a turreted baronial estate now occupied by an Innes Catto. In planning our trip, I had corresponded with Mr. Catto, who graciously consented to show us around the property upon our arrival. He also produced a detailed history of the Chivas family.

"The family Schevez was of Norman origin," the history began. "They arrived in England in the army of William the Conqueror and led their contingent at (the battle of) Hastings (1066). Their arrival in Scotland dates from the reign of David I (1124–1153)."

On assuming the crown of Scotland, the history continued, David invited the Norman barons who had settled in England to come to Scotland. These Norman barons first settled in the southern districts on grants of land given to them by the king. The process gradually spread northwards and, in the 14th century, the Schevez family assumed ownership of the Barony of Schevez in the parish of Tarves, East Aberdeenshire.

But what did the name Schevez and its variant spellings mean? I wanted to know. The family history yielded a plausible answer:

"The name Schevez is of territorial origin. The Celtic peoples, who named so many of the physical features of Scotland, gave the name 'seamhas,' meaning 'prosperity,' to the territory that afterwards became known as the Barony of Schivas."

This was a real find, a major breakthrough in the search for our origins. It was what I had been looking for, that is, from whence came the name and the meaning behind it. It also would explain the variations in spelling over the centuries: "seamhas" sounds like it could easily have evolved to Chivas, Schivas, Schevez, Sheves—or Shevis.

More than any other document, the family history lit up the past and brought to life many of my distant relatives, including one William Scheves. According to the history, William Scheves was named archbishop of St. Andrews in 1478 and is described as "one of the most remarkable men of his time. Educated at Louvain (Belgium's oldest university), he made rapid progress in theology, astrology and medicine," the report said. "It is said that he had scarcely his equal in Britain and France.

"A great favorite with King James III (1460–1488), William Scheves was frequently chosen as ambassador to foreign countries where his ability and learning did much to enhance the reputation of his native Scotland."

(Five of Scheves's seals as archbishop—along with those of other archbishops of St. Andrews—are on display in the visitor's center at St. Andrews Cathedral, which we visited on our last day in St. Andrews.)

We mulled all this over as we left the House of Schivas for Fraserburgh, where my father grew up. Once there, we clambered over huge rocks at Kinnaird Head where he played as a boy. We also took photos of his Charlotte Street home, which, like so many Scottish homes, was built of granite to last forever.

With dusk coming on, we headed west for Inverness to position ourselves for the ferry trip to Orkney the next day. We stayed the night in Inverness, but decided to forgo the trip north because of time limitations. Instead, we drove south for a tour of the battlefield at Culloden where in 1746 English troops crushed the rebellious Charles Edward Stuart and his followers, forever ending the House of Stuart's hopes of regaining the British throne.

We also stopped at Urquhart Castle on Loch Ness near Drumnadrochit, one of the largest castles in Scotland, offering splendid views up and down the loch. Just as we approached the 500-year-old castle's remains, a double rainbow appeared out of the mist.

Andrew had not forgotten about playing golf at St. Andrews, every golfer's dream. Nor had I. And so, with only two days left in our Scottish itinerary, we returned to the same bed and breakfast place we had stayed at earlier in St. Andrews.

The renowned Old Course, where the game was first played, around 1400 A.D., was fully booked until late October, but Maggie Wilson, our resourceful B & B hostess, rung up the Strathtyrum—one of five other courses managed by the St. Andrews Links Trust—and secured a 10 a.m. starting time for us there. Andy carded a 75 on the 18-hole course where par is 69; my score is a state secret.

At Heathrow, while awaiting our flight home, each of us wrote a list of the highlights of our Scottish tour. Both of us put playing golf at St. Andrews first, followed by the House of Schivas visit. Later, as the giant 747 lifted from the ground, I remembered Maggie Wilson's husband Tom calling out to us as we drove away: "Haste ye back!"

I'm almost certain we will return.

SUBURBAN SPRAWL: A NATIONAL ISSUE

While the chief contenders in the year 2000 presidential election race have already emerged—Vice President Al Gore seems the odds-on favorite to run against Texas Governor George W. Bush—the issues have yet to become clear.

One issue has already come to the fore, however, and is demanding increased attention from the candidates: what to do about suburban sprawl. Republican Bush has yet to clarify exactly where he stands on the issue. Gore has been more forthcoming, and has made the issue a cornerstone of his campaign.

Both candidates are against suburban sprawl, of course. It's one of those "mom-and-apple-pie" issues. After all, who could be for traffic congestion and cookie-cutter construction projects that have made so much of the United States look the same? But only Gore so far has announced specifics of an anti-sprawl program.

Early this year, the vice president outlined the Clinton administration's plans to curb urban sprawl and ease traffic congestion by boosting federal spending on open-space land purchases, transportation programs, and regional planning by $10 billion or more. Known as the Livable Communities initiative, the plan is aimed at preserving critical wildlife habitats and providing permanent financing for farms, city parks and other green spaces across the country.

"All our communities face a preservation challenge as they grow and green space shrinks," President Clinton said in his 1999 State of the Union address.

Political observers say Gore's concern over urban sprawl resonates so well with the American people that it gives him an edge with the electorate.

In most U.S. presidential elections, the overriding issue has been the state of the economy—how well is it doing and where is it going? In the 2000 general election, however, the economy is going so well, many voters are more concerned about "livability" and quality-of-life issues.

People have railed against rampant, uncontrolled growth for years. The difference between now and then is that enough people now appear to be so frustrated with the perils of suburban living they're willing to take action to build better suburbs—a major step forward in the anti-sprawl movement taking hold across the country.

James Redfield, in his book, *The Celestine Prophecy*, while not addressing urban sprawl *per se*, writes of "a kind of renaissance in consciousness, occurring very slowly, that could explain what is going on in suburbia today.

"It's not religious in nature, but it is spiritual," Redfield says. He attributes this renewal of consciousness to "the number of individuals having this awareness at the same time." It's what "I think of as a critical mass," he says.

Steve Twomey, writing in *The Washington Post*, said that "few topics are sizzling hotter than the quality of suburban life and growth, as if there's been some grand jelling of frustration with traffic and blandness even among suburbanites."

Twomey noted that the National Trust for Historic Preservation, which has joined the debate over uncontrolled growth, counted 240 anti-sprawl initiatives on state and local ballots last year, and 29 governors speaking out about uncontrolled growth this year. Congress has joined the fray, too, and has held hearings on the problem.

Gore, too, sees the problems besetting Earth in a spiritual framework. In an interview with this writer shortly after publication of his book, *Earth in the Balance: Ecology and the Human Spirit*, Gore said he believes the global environmental crisis reflects "an outer manifestation of an inner crisis that is, for lack of a better word, spiritual."

"We've somehow come to the conclusion that we're above it all, disconnected from the physical world and living in the world of the intellect instead," he said. "It is this separation from each other, from other communities, and from the ecological web of life that leads to the spiritual crisis that I refer to in the book.

"Global warming, depletion of ozone, destruction of the forest land, and all the other ecological crises are really just symptoms of the deeper, underlying spiritual crisis. But it can be healed, and it must be healed."

Gore spells out a prescription for what ails the world. His strongest recommendation is a worldwide effort to stabilize the world's rising population. "No goal is more crucial to healing the global environment," he says.

Gore also calls for steps to protect biodiversity—plants and animals living together with humans—which is essential to a healthy Earth. As matters now stand, industrial civilization and the planet's ecological system are on a collision course, Gore warned. "The signs are all around us," and none is more visible than urban sprawl, he says.

Speaking to a Brookings Institution audience, Gore said that "over the last 30 years, bad planning has too often distorted our towns and landscapes out of all recognition."

"Too many places are burdened by an ugliness that leaves us with a quiet sense of sadness. The burden is national. No state has escaped it.

"The problem which we suffer in too many of our cities, suburbs, and rural areas is made up of so many different pieces that until recently it has been a problem that lacked a name. 'Sprawl' hardly does justice to it."

One important aspect of the problem is that while population is on the increase, the amount of land being used for urbanized purposes—office buildings, shopping centers, houses and parking lots—is rising twice as fast in some areas, such as Washington, D.C. Concomitantly, the infrastructure—water and sewer lines, public transportation, schools and particularly roads—is not keeping up with jobs. The result is gridlock.

"The jobs are in the suburbs, but much of the labor force is in the city," Witold Rybczynski, a professor of architecture at the University of Pennsylvania, said in a *Wall Street Journal* article. "New transportation links are required between the two."

According to *The Economist*, traffic jams in Atlanta have been so entangled that babies have been born in traffic and some desperate drivers have left their cars to relieve themselves behind roadside bushes.

Unfortunately, the administration's proposal for more livable communities has met with a chilly reception in Congress. Committees in both the House and the Senate have voted to cut deeply into Clinton's request for appropriations.

The Gore-Clinton people are not anti-growth writ large. In fact, they believe towns and cities can protect the environment and improve the local economy at the same time. What Gore seeks is orderly growth; his position is that as communities become more livable and less congested, they will have the advantage of attracting more businesses and jobholders.

Meanwhile, the urban sprawl that afflicts the nation continues to elbow wildlife from their natural habitat. Deer, coyotes, bear, Canada geese, the red cockaded woodpecker, Colorado's greenback trout, the dusky seaside sparrow, and the Maryland darter are among the losers. With no place to go, they bound across highways and into people's backyards in search of food and water, frequently injuring themselves or causing harm to people.

This year's drought has brought out larger than usual numbers of wildlife, especially in the Northeast. Coyotes—normally found only in the West and Appalachia—now have been sighted in every state, according to *The New York Times.*

There have been some winners, however, the most conspicuous being the American bald eagle. On the eve of the nation's 1999 Independence Day celebration, President Clinton announced plans to remove the bird from the nation's endangered species list next year.

Once there were half a million or more bald eagles in the United States. As a result of widespread hunting, use of the toxic pesticide DDT, and loss of prey and habitat, their number fell to 417 nesting pairs by 1963.

When DDT was banned and the bird placed on the endangered species list, the bald eagle recovered from its dramatic slide to the point where there are now nearly 6,000 breeding pairs in the continental United States.

"The American bald eagle is back," Interior Secretary Bruce Babbitt said. But other wildlife remains threatened or endangered. "There are still a lot of species teetering on the brink of extinction."

According to the U.S. Fish and Wildlife Service (USFWS), there were 357 animal species and 568 different plants listed as endangered at the end of April 1999. Another 123 animal species and 135 plant species were on the department's threatened list, for a total of 1,183 wildlife species desperately in need of protection. Significantly, only 10 species have been removed from the endangered list since it was established in 1973; four recovered and six were determined to be extinct.

During the Clinton administration, USFWS has added an average of 85 plant and animal species to the list. In nearly every instance, human activity posed the threat.

"Habitat loss is the number-one reason why they are sliding toward endangerment," the USFWS said. The agency said it plans to initiate its protocol for delisting 20 to 25 plant and animal species over the next three years.

While Babbitt said he is heartened by the "spectacular successes we've had protecting the salmon, wolves, peregrine falcon and the gray whale," the nation's endangered plants and animals for the most part are fighting a losing battle. With virtually no control over urban sprawl, the wildlife so essential for ecological balance could eventually become extinct.

In various parts of western United States, bears, mountain lions, coyotes, and black-tailed deer are the most pressing problem; in the eastern and midwestern parts of the country, the most visible problems are with the white-tailed deer and Canada geese. In every case, their enemy is man, relentlessly taking over their territory with backhoe and earthmover.

Deer, which have grown less timid and unafraid of humans, are increasing in number despite urban sprawl. More and more deer sightings are occurring throughout the country, especially in the Middle Atlantic states. Tens of thousands of deer are said to roam the Washington suburbs in search of food and water.

"There's no question development is having an impact on the deer," Roy Geiger, a wildlife biologist with the National Wildlife Federation in Vienna, Virginia, said in an interview with this writer. "Development and highway construction disrupt the natural travel flow of deer—the pathways and routes they ordinarily use.

"Let's say you have a thick area of woods at Point A where the deer live and they want to get to a stream at Point B, and you lay an expressway through the center of those two points," Geiger said.

"They're not going to go around the expressway to get to the stream. They're creatures of habit: they're going to maintain that traditional pathway and cross the road. You have the breaking-up of their whole natural habitat."

Deer sightings are so common these days they're hardly a topic of conversation anymore. Nearly everyone has seen one or more of them by the roadside.

Just the same, as I gazed out my bedroom window in northern Virginia one day this summer, I was surprised to see a doe and her fawn foraging 50 feet away in my backyard. I got out the binoculars for a closer look, and tried to figure why *my* backyard. And then it came to me: they were attracted to the green apples on the ground, as well as by the grassy lawn and nearby water pond.

Mine is not the only house where uninvited deer have come calling. Even the White House has not escaped visits from them. In April, three apparently disoriented does wandered into downtown Washington and wound up banging themselves against the black wrought-iron fence that surrounds the executive mansion.

One was caught tangled in the fence, while another jumped into the courtyard of the Treasury Building next door, and hurt itself. District of Columbia animal control officers tranquilized the two, then euthanized them because of the severity of their injuries.

The third doe survived after being trapped in a courtyard near the New Executive Office Building; it was taken to Gaithersburg in suburban Maryland to recover and eventually released.

Besides chewing up gardens and shrubbery, wayward deer cause an estimated half-million vehicle accidents a year, killing 100 people and injuring thousands more, the Insurance Information Institute says.

Deer pose another problem. When a deer is killed in a highway collision, removing the carcass can be expensive. Michigan's Oakland County pays $12.50 to $25 in landfill-disposal fees per deer. In 1998, the county had 1,668 vehicle-deer collisions, fourth highest among the state's 83 counties.

All of which makes it easy to understand why some jurisdictions are taking steps to reduce the deer population. Lengthening the hunting season so hunters can shoot and kill them is growing in popularity. But the deer have shown themselves to adapt well to hunting, and in all likelihood will continue to thrive and multiply.

Another creature caught in the crosshairs of urban sprawl is the Canada goose. Its numbers have risen dramatically throughout the country in recent years. Once an almost entirely migratory species that bred and spent their summers in Canada, huge flocks of geese have now taken up year-round residence in various parts of the United States, especially the East.

While beautiful and awesome to look at in their V-formation flights, the birds have drawn the ire of homeowners, golf course managers, businesses, and airport managers for the damage and nuisance they say the birds cause.

The main complaint against the geese is they defecate on lawns, lakefronts, bodies of water and other areas frequented by humans. Responding to complaints, at least four states have embarked on a catch-and-kill program to solve the problem.

In 1997, the Wildlife Division of the U.S. Department of Agriculture, with help from Virginia authorities, rounded up and killed 1,548 Canada geese at 16 locations, mostly in northern Virginia.

The next year, animal-rights groups led by the Humane Society of the United States won a split decision from a federal judge when they sued the government to prevent a recurrence of the killings.

The judge agreed to allow the killings only at Dulles International and Reagan National airports where the geese are considered a possible threat to aviation; 155 birds were killed last year. In 1999, the same groups sued to stop the slaughter but the judge declined to render a decision, leaving both sides unhappy.

The animal-protection groups acknowledge that the geese are messy but should not be killed just for that. They say there are effective, humane, non-lethal ways of dealing with the geese, including habitat modification, harassment techniques, and using trained border collies to keep them away from grassy expanses such as golf courses.

The plight of the Canada geese and the deer points up the problem of sprawl in suburban America. Deer and geese populations are growing rapidly at the same time the human population spirals. It comes down to a struggle over resources, a struggle the deer and the geese and other wildlife are unlikely to win.

But some adjustment in the relationship between man and nature is desperately needed to bring Earth into balance, to where there's room for all God's creatures.

CHINA TODAY: A TRAVELER'S MUST-SEE

"If you fail to reach the Great Wall,
"You are not a man."

So goes a Chinese saying, and a lot of foreign tourists are traveling to China these days to prove their manhood, it seems.

Many of the visitors are retired Americans with the resources to make the long trip—a tiring 14-hour flight from Washington Dulles International Airport to Beijing. They're among the 78-million overseas arrivals expected to visit the People's Republic of China by the end of 2001.

Domestic tourism also is booming. It's estimated that 750-million Chinese will tour their homeland by the end of the year.

Unquestionably the big draw, the Great Wall wends its way across northern China from Gansu province to the Yellow Sea. Built 2,000 years ago by China's first emperor, Qin Shi Huangdi, to keep out invaders, successive invasions by northern nomads proved the wall to be of little military value.

As the Great Wall lost its military importance, it became a historic relic much beloved of sightseers, such as the small group of Americans of which I was one who journeyed to China to see it for themselves.

The Great Wall is the best preserved of China's many historical and cultural relics, an awesome structure undulating across the country's steep terrain like a guardian dragon. In some ways, it reminds me of Hadrian's Wall, erected (A.D. 122–26) across the width of Great Britain by the Roman Emperor Hadrian to keep northern raiders from invading the south.

There are major differences, of course. Hadrian's Wall was built on a much smaller scale than the Great Wall of China. Britain's wall was

73.5 miles long, and only fragments of it remain today, whereas the Great Wall was 1,500 miles in length and is relatively well preserved.

But both barriers had the same objective: keep people out.

The Chinese boast that the Great Wall, which averages 25 feet in height, is the only man-made structure visible from outer space. They are justifiably proud of it, and claim it as the eighth man-made wonder of the world—an utterly believable declaration if you've seen it in person.

The Badaling section of the wall, about 50 miles from the center of Beijing, China's capital, is the most visited stretch of the Great Wall. Swarms of visitors climb its uneven steps, many pausing to rest along the way.

The climb is not for the faint of heart. The wall is steeper than it appears in films or books. A 64-year-old member of our group found himself unable to walk farther than the length of a football field before calling it quits.

Another test of a tourist's endurance is surviving the pack of vendors hawking baseball caps and T-shirts proclaiming "I Climbed the Great Wall," fake jewelry, books and other items. I found them more aggressive than those pushing souvenirs and other goods at the border crossing in Tijuana, Mexico.

Pleading, begging and bargaining, they literally get in your face, shouting "how much," "one dollah," "one dollah," shoving us as we walked away. But this is all part of the atmospherics, and fails to deter the thousands of visitors drawn annually to China's number-one tourist attraction.

Travel to China is not uncommon these days. Huge jumbo jet aircraft routinely bring tourists from all over the world to this vast country, depositing them in the big cities of Beijing, Guangzhou, Xi'an, Nanjing and Shanghai where breathtaking sights await them.

It's not just tourists arriving in large numbers, though. There is also a steady flow of traders from the West seeking new markets for their goods and services in the world's most populous country. Americans lead the pack.

China has undergone an economic revolution since the government adopted a degree of democratic capitalism.

According to the State Statistics Bureau, China's economy grew 8.2 percent during the first three quarters of 2000. The country continued to see strong growth in exports during that period, much of it due to trade with the United States.

China's entry into the World Trade Organization (WTO), now expected to occur in mid-2001, could help spur another economic revolution for the nation. The aim of the WTO, which is strongly supported by the United States, is to reduce trade barriers among countries of the world.

As a result, tariffs will fall, forcing Chinese firms to either compete with, or be absorbed by, Western businesses. Also, China's farmers likely will be forced to revolutionize their ancient farming methods in the face of rising agricultural imports from the West.

Meanwhile, tourism remains a staple of China's economy. An estimated 55.1-million foreign tourists visited China between January and August of 2000—a 16.5-percent increase over the same period last year. According to the China National Tourism Administration, total tourism revenue will amount to US$ 54.3 billion in 2001.

While the Great Wall of China tops the list of prime tourist attractions, there are countless others—among them, the Forbidden City, Tiananmen Square, the Summer Palace, and the Giant Panda Zoo.

Without question, the underground army of terra cotta warriors and horses in Xi'an—built 2,000 years ago to guard China's first emperor on his trip into the hereafter—is the most spectacular sight after the Great Wall. Some people might reverse the order but none would deny the magnitude of the undertaking, one of the great archaeological finds of the 20th century.

Discovered by accident in March 1974 by a farmer digging a well, Qin Shi Huangdi's mausoleum leaves visitors slack-jawed at the immensity of the find. At first, only some broken pieces of pottery were unearthed. But as further excavation occurred, thousands of lifelike warriors and horses were found.

In three pits, archaeologists found some 2,000 life-sized human figures made of baked earth, including chariot warriors, cavalry and infantry members and others arranged in good order and looking like a massive imperial army.

Calculating the arrangement density of the unearthed figures, archaeologists believe there are about 6,000 terra cotta army members and a large number of bronze arms yet embedded in the ground.

In the 26 years since their discovery, exploration and excavation of the vaults have never stopped. Two years after the discovery, the Chinese government built an arched structure resembling an aircraft hangar to protect the exposed soldiers and horses from the weather.

The find created a worldwide sensation, and boosted China's tourist industry immensely. In his book, *Riding the Iron Rooster: By Train Through China*, (G.P. Putnam's Sons, New York, 1988), writer Paul Theroux quotes his Chinese guide as saying that until the discovery no tourists came to Xi'an:

"We never saw Americans. They started coming after the terra-cotta army was found. Then people were very interested. More and more things were unearthed. People wanted to see these things."

According to Theroux, "The warriors are the one masterpiece in China that has not been repainted, faked and further vandalized."

Many of those who travel to China today are older people. At breakfast and dinner, you see a lot of gray heads. In the Gang of Eight, as we called ourselves, all but one person was retired, including a 71-year-old Floridian who used a walker to get around.

Crossing city streets can be hazardous, particularly at rush hour when a chaos of cars, buses, trucks and bicycles descends upon wary pedestrians. As Karen, a member of our group put it after a close call with a Peugeot

While there are more cars on the roads than just a few years ago, still they are hard to come by for the average citizen. One of the smallest vehicles sells for over $50,000. For that reason, China remains a nation of bicyclists.

It's amazing how dexterous are the bikers and the size of the loads they carry on their two-wheelers. I saw one man lug a full-length sofa on the back of his bike.

The Chinese are an environmentally conscious people. They work at it. Air pollution is down, and there is an awareness on the part of the populace that everyone needs to pitch in. At our hotel in Shanghai, for instance, guests were left the following notice on their pillow:

"In our effort to contribute to the preservation of the environment and reduce the pollution caused by detergents, we will replace your bed sheets and pillow cases every three days (instead of every day). If you put this card on the bed, we will be pleased to replace them with fresh ones for you. Thank you for caring for our home!"

Ours was a very successful trip. Packaged by Regent China Tours of Tampa, Florida, the 10-day trip was competitively priced, included accommodations at 4- and 5-star hotels, all meals, transfers, and English-speaking guides.

The trip's only down side remains the same for most Americans—the long, exhausting 14-hour flights to and from China. But that may be speeded up if a joint Russian-Canadian study bears fruit.

The study found that opening air traffic routes over the North Pole and across Siberia to thousands of commercial flights is feasible, and could shave more than three hours off existing transpacific routes from the U.S. East Coast.

The Cold War put development of such routes on hold in the past. Now that the conflict has ended and long-range planes like the Boeing 747–400 and the Airbus A-340 have come on line, the polar routes could make the flight to China more comfortable.

A RIDE THROUGH MOSBY'S CONFEDERACY

America's deadliest war—the four-year Civil War that claimed over 600,000 lives—continues to fascinate thousands of people across the land.

As the warm days of summer come upon us and tourists increasingly take to the highways, the number of Americans expected to visit Civil War sites is expected to soar—particularly in Virginia where some 60 percent of all Civil War battles were fought. An estimated 519 engagements between Union and Confederate troops took place in Virginia; the next highest number, 298, occurred in Tennessee.

Northern Virginians, as well as Marylanders, won't have to go far to visit these historic places and byways. In some cases, they literally need go little farther than their own back yard.

Only 30 yards or so from my house, for instance, there flows a trickle of a stream along which at some point contending cavalrymen in the war paused during the fighting to water their mounts.

Appropriately named Horsepen Run, the four-mile stream near Herndon is "more than likely" the same today as it was 135 years ago, according to Robin Worcester, a geographer in the United States Geological Survey's (USGS) national mapping division in Reston.

There's no telling what or how many, if any, military engagements took place on the banks of Horsepen Run—its name rarely appears in Civil War records—but we know from his memoirs that a certain Confederate cavalry officer by the name of John Singleton Mosby chased a Union band of horsemen to the edge of the stream one day in 1863.

"They exceeded us in number," Mosby writes. "They scampered away, with us close behind them. Soon they got to Horsepen Run, which was booming from the melting snows, and the foremost man plunged into the stream."

Mosby—a guerrilla fighter who made a career of raiding Union strongholds in northern Virginia, causing general disruption and disarray—was known as the "Gray Ghost" for his hit-and-run raids, most of which came in the night.

One such raid, this one in broad daylight, took place in what is now downtown Herndon. With no loss to his men, Mosby attacked a Vermont cavalry unit, capturing four officers, 21 enlisted men, all their weapons and horses.

Mosby and his marauding band were early forerunners of the Vietcong, you might say: farmers by day, soldiers by night. They seemed to be everywhere in northern Virginia, so controlling the region with their lightning-like strikes that it became known as Mosby's Confederacy.

For all his exploits and derring-do, Mosby is relatively unknown to most Americans; he has been overshadowed by Robert E. Lee, Stonewall Jackson, J.E.B. Stuart and other Confederate household names. Serious Civil War historians, however, give Colonel Mosby his due, and rank him as one of the great tacticians of the war. In and around

Fauquier, Fairfax and Loudoun counties, where Mosby mostly operated, he and his men attained near-legend status. Lee, the top Confederate commander, noted that in about a year's time Mosby's unit had killed, wounded or captured some 1,200 Union troops with the loss of about 20 of his own men, and taken some 1,600 horses and mules.

But that was long ago. Many Americans are just now beginning to educate themselves about the man. Reenactment of Mosby skirmishes, the newly formed John Singleton Mosby Heritage Area group, additional highway markers highlighting his successes, and guided tours of "Mosbyland" have combined to raise the partisan leader's profile.

On a splendid day in May, 34 history buffs boarded a bus in front of the historic Freeman House in Vienna, Virginia and set off on an all-day guided tour of Civil War sites associated with the adventurous Mosby. Historic Vienna, Inc., sponsored the trip, a 110-mile swing through Fairfax, Aldie, Middleburg, Marshall, Atoka, and Warren-ton—towns and places that figured prominently in Mosby's career.

James M. Moyer and Thomas J. Evans, co-authors of the book, *Mosby's Confederacy* were the tour guides; the two have conducted the tour 16 times. Moyer is a Fairfax County physical-education teacher; Evans is retired from the U.S. Army Corps of Engineers.

The Freeman House changed hands frequently during the Civil War. Union officers were quartered there and kept their horses in the cellar; Confederate forces used the building as a hospital.

Before the bus pulled away, a permanent marker citing the role of the Freeman House during the war was unveiled in front of the build-ing. The marker recounts the "long history of a house and a place which touched the lives of countless persons during the time it was caught in the conflict," Paul D. Snodgrass, president of Historic Vienna, Inc., said.

First stop on the tour was the Truro Episcopal Church rectory in Fairfax, which served as the headquarters for General Edwin Stough-ton, the Union area commander. It was in this building, on the night of March 8,1863, that Mosby penetrated Union lines of 3,000 men and captured Stoughton in bed, taking him, 40 officers and men, and 58 horses through Union lines to Confederate territory. The feat brought Mosby immediate attention from higher-ups, including Lee, who gave him wide latitude the rest of the war.

The bus tour followed U.S. Route 50, a portion of which is named the John S. Mosby Highway, to the village of Aldie where on July 6, 1864 Mosby and his band scored a major victory over units of the 13th New York Cavalry and the 2nd Massachusetts Cavalry. The battle occurred about one half-mile east of Mount Zion Baptist Church, a frequent stopover for Union troops. Eighty Union soldiers were killed, wounded or captured in the fighting. Mosby, though greatly outnum-bered, lost one of his men; six others were wounded.

Built in 1851, the church still stands albeit in somewhat rundown condition. Normally closed to the public, the church opened its doors to the tour group. The nearby cemetery contains the remains of 12 Union men and 13 Confederates. The church has been inactive since 1980; church trustees have agreed to turn the building over to Loudoun County in the coming year as a historic site commemorating the county's rich Civil War history.

As the bus sped through the beautiful Virginia countryside—past Kent Farms, owned by the estate of the late Jack Kent Cooke, the former owner of the Washington Redskins—Moyer and Evans pointed to other Mosby sites: the Red Fox Inn in Middleburg, where Mosby met with Jeb Stuart just prior to the pivotal battle at Gettysburg; Atoka, where Mosby's unit was organized on June 10,1863; Lakeland, the house in which Mosby was critically wounded in 1864, and Marshall, where Mosby disbanded his guerrilla unit on April 21,1865.

In farewell remarks to his men, Mosby said that "the vision we have cherished for a free and independent country has vanished, and the country is now the spoil of a conqueror. I disband your organization in preference to surrender to our enemies."

In Warrenton, where Mosby had a thriving law practice after the war, tour members visited the gravesite of the colorful Confederate leader. Members of his immediate family are buried there as well as a number of his partisan band.

After lunch, on the return trip to Vienna, a somewhat subdued group chewed on what they had seen and learned about Mosby that day.

Corinna Hodges, who lives in Hanover, Maryland, near Baltimore-Washington International Airport, said that the highlight of the tour for her was the visit to Mount Zion Church.

"We had been there before, but could look inside only through the shutters," said Hodges, who works in the U.S. Geological Survey's national mapping division in Reston. "It was neat to be in something that old."

Carl Lukac of Vienna, who recently retired as an astronomer at the U.S. Naval Observatory in Washington, said he sympathizes with the

Confederacy's "Lost Cause," even though he grew up and was educated in the North. He is an active participant in the reenactment of Civil War battles, a popular hobby these days, especially in northern Virginia and Maryland. Reenactors stage mock battles, using smoke bombs and firing reproduction muskets.

"I've wanted to make this tour for about three years now," said Lukac, who has lived in Virginia for about 35 years. "I'm realizing that we have someone in our own neighborhood who's contributed quite a bit to the Civil War, and I wanted to know more about him."

Some social commentators contend that the Civil War is still unfinished business in the hearts and minds of many in the South who continue to believe in what Mosby stood and fought for. But Lukac has a different take on the matter:

"I don't think they're still fighting the war," he said. "I think they just don't want to forget the war."

STEDMAN GRAHAM: THE WIND IN OPRAH'S SAILS

Oprah Winfrey, queen of the daytime television talk shows, is one of those people who seem to know early in life where they're going.

At the age of 12, while visiting her father in Nashville, Winfrey was paid $500 to speak at a church. "I told my daddy then and there that I planned to be very famous," she said. "I wanted to be paid to talk."

That she reached her goal is self-evident. Her *Oprah Winfrey Show* has made her a household word and one of the highest-paid entertainers in the country. She has everything money can buy—a condo on Chicago's Gold Coast, a ranch in Telluride, Colorado, an oceanside dwelling in Miami, and much more.

But for much of her life she lacked that which money cannot buy: the happiness that a loving, trusting relationship can bring. In a word, she lacked a soulmate—someone who would be there when she needed him, through good times and bad.

Oprah had just about given up hope of ever finding Mr. Right. And then one day she found him in the 6-foot-6 presence of Stedman Graham, Jr. Her life has never been the same since.

"I think what happened is what I read about in all the women's magazines," she told ABC's Barbara Walters. "They say if you stop looking, you can find it."

From everything she has said about Graham, her "significant other" since 1986, the Chicago businessman has been a steadying influence and a perfect complement for her.

"He is one of the kindest and most patient men I have ever known," she says, which is "one of the reasons we're still together. And he is honorable. Like my father, just honorable." (*The Uncommon Wisdom of Oprah Winfrey: A Portrait in Her Own Words*, Carol Publishing Group)

Psychologists might look at Graham as a father figure, reminding her of her father, Vernon Winfrey, who kept her on the straight and narrow during her growing-up years.

They might also note with interest that she and Stedman have never married, even though they've been going together for 15 years. Could it have anything to do with the fact her biological parents never married? Who knows. It is only speculation. "We'll get married when both of us are ready." she has said.

Who is this Stedman Graham, Jr., this rock of support for the nation's number-one talk-show host? What do they have in common?

For starters, they share similar interests and beliefs. They're both shrewd business people. Both are positive-minded individuals, exponents of the human-potential movement. They're into "empowerment," especially for impoverished black youths.

Graham has been highly successful in business. He is president and chief executive officer of Stedman Graham & Associates, a Chicago-based sports-management, marketing and consulting firm.

He is also the founder of Athletes Against Drugs, a nonprofit organization created to combat substance abuse and to promote youth leadership. In his spare time, he wrote a *New York Times* bestseller—*You Can Make It Happen: A Nine-Step Plan for Success*—that he dedicated to Oprah:

"Without her influence and her belief in me, I doubt that I ever would have discovered true freedom and what it means. Her knowledge and understanding of the world has added so much to my life. I shall always be grateful to her for helping to fill the hole in my heart."

Graham is three years older than Oprah. Born in 1951 in Whiteboro, New Jersey, an African American community surrounded by a predominantly white county; he was one of six children, two of whom were developmentally disabled. Their father was a painter and contractor, his mother a homemaker.

Because of his height and prowess as a basketball player, Stedman starred on his high-school team. His athletic skills enabled him to get a college education. He earned a Bachelor of Arts degree in social work at Hardin-Simmons University in Texas and a master's degree in education at Ball State University in Indiana.

Basketball was his passion; he dreamed of playing professionally. But, he has said, he lacked the self-esteem and support he needed to go for it. He married soon after graduating from Hardin-Simmons in 1974. The following year, he became a father when his daughter Wendy was born. He and Glenda later divorced. Some say he has been marriage-shy ever since and that this explains why he and Oprah haven't married.

He played basketball in Europe for three years, averaging 30 points a game, but was unable to break into the National Basketball Association at home—one of the biggest disappointments in his life, he told an interviewer.

Sports remained a big part of Graham's life, however. In addition to founding Athletes Against Drugs and Stedman & Associates, he wrote a column for *Inside Sports* magazine. In 1994, Graham was named director of George Washington University's Forum for Sport and Event Management and Marketing in Washington, D.C.

Graham's romance with Oprah began in 1985. Cautious at first because of doubts about herself, Oprah stood him up. But after he called again, she went out with him. As time went on, their relationship blossomed.

"Stedman is ideal for me," she has said. "He's my number-one fan, and he isn't jealous of my success."

In an interview with *Essence* magazine, Oprah said "he knows who he is." She added: "I am thrilled that I have discovered this in a black man."

Graham's willingness to stay out of the limelight is an indication of his independence and his inner security. But it hasn't always been easy being the boyfriend of a megastar, as Graham acknowledged in a first-person article in the March 1997 issue of *McCall's* magazine.

One day, as he was walking along a Chicago street, a construction worker greeted him with, "Hey, Oprah's boyfriend, how's it going?"

At one time, being seen only as Oprah Winfrey's boyfriend might have made him flinch and given the worker a cold stare, he said. But because he had overcome the low self-esteem and negative racial images in his youth and family circumstances, he let the remark pass.

Instead, he shook the man's hand and struck up a conversation with him. "At the end of our conversation, he called me Mr. Graham," he said, an altogether healthier appellation than the "Mr. Oprah" title others had given him.

Graham said the catalyst that spurred him into a better understanding of himself was his relationship with Oprah. As Oprah became a national celebrity, he said, he'd been feeling increasingly uncomfortable.

"I was an unequal partner, at least in the eyes of the public," he said. "The pain of dealing with this issue forced me to look inside myself." But without Oprah's help and understanding, he might not have come to understand what had been holding him back from a fuller life, he said.

"Oprah forced me to confront my insecurities," he said. "She tried to make me understand that the roots of my pain were in my past. I stewed over her words for a long time before I acknowledged she was right."

One of the questions they are often asked is, when are they going to get married. Interestingly, Graham did not discuss the matter in his *Mc Call's* article. For her part, Oprah has said she's "sick," sick, "sick" of the question.

In 1997, when the couple was interviewed on *The Gayle King Show,* members of the audience posed the marriage question to them. They had become engaged in 1992.

Graham had joined King in her Hartford, Connecticut studio while Winfrey joined them by satellite from Chicago. The 1997 interview marked the first time the couple had been interviewed on a talk show together.

Winfrey replied that they had no immediate plans to tie the knot.

"I think we have deep love and caring for each other and respect," she said. "Every day we get asked a question about when are you getting married, and I say it works so well the way it is, I wouldn't want to mess it up.

"I think that for us, this is what works right now, which is not to say that we never would get married."

Oprah said that what makes their relationship work is honesty and the commitment they have for each other. "He is one person who would tell me the truth…and I would tell him the truth."

Another thing that makes the relationship work, she said, is "we laugh a lot."

King is an old friend of Oprah's. "She keeps me grounded," Winfrey said. Graham encourages the friendship:

"I think it's therapeutic for Oprah to have someone she can talk to and tell everything about her day and everything about her week."

Besides King, Oprah's inner circle includes her attorney Jeffrey Jacobs, who has guided her career; Bill and Camille Cosby; Barbara

Walters; composer and producer Quincy Jones, and the black American author Maya Angelou.

Because of the vicissitudes of their schedules, theirs is a long-distance romance. Yet they manage to see each other and to stay in touch.

Together, in the fall of 1999, they taught a course in leadership at Northwestern University's Kellogg Graduate School of Management. The course, "Dynamics of Leadership," which they jointly developed, was designed to help business students enhance their abilities to lead effectively.

Graham's definition of ethical leadership is consistency over time in matters such as honesty and hard work, and setting a good example—a code that Oprah embraces as well.

For a while, in 1994, there was talk that Oprah—the highest-paid daytime TV talk show host in America—might leave television to take on new challenges. Since then, she has branched out into producing films and TV specials, launched an on-air book club and a women's magazine, and would seem to have enough on her plate—for now at least.

For someone this busy, it's hard to imagine there's also room for marriage. But if there's to be one, Stedman is the likely candidate. He's a success in his own right, secure enough to live with the incandescent Oprah, and still be his own man.

0-595-24604-4